UNVEILING THE MESSIAH

IN THE FALL FEASTS

By Tekoa Manning

Also By Tekoa Manning

Walter: The Homeless Man, a novel

Polishing Jade, a novel

Thirsting for Water, a devotional

Jumping for Joy in the Midst of Sorrow, a devotional

The Spirit of Leviathan, Jezebel, and Athaliah, a teaching book.

Emmitt's Dinosaur, a children's book.

Unveiling the Messiah in the Spring Feasts

Unveiling the Messiah in the Fall Feasts

Unmasking the Unseen Book Series

Satan Unmasked, Book One

Spirits Unveiled, Book Two

Wolves Unseen, Book Three

King Revealed, Book Four

ISBN-13: 978-1-961773-14-1 (Manning the Gate Publishing LLC)

Unveiling the Messiah in the Fall Feasts

Editor – Jo Fouts Zausch

Cover by Lynette Marie Smith
Graphic Design & Marketing

Table of Contents

Introduction

Many books have been written with much wisdom concerning the Holy One's feasts/appointed times. There are multiple blogs and articles on the feasts as well as traditions on how to keep them, from a Jewish and Christian perspective. This book will offer more understanding on the Messiah in each feast day and how to navigate this new knowledge in your life without bondage. I also expound on the coming of the Messiah and both the light and darkness hidden in the Fall Feast Days.

I write concerning the voice of the prophets of old and spend more time and attention on the prophetic passages concerning the seven feasts listed in the Tanakh (Old Testament) and the times we are living in. I believe we are approaching difficult times, but if we look to the heavens concerning the Holy One's calendar, we can be prepared. Psalm 19 states that the heavens declare our Father's glory and the heavens have a voice:

> The heavens declare the glory of God, and the sky shows His handiwork. Day to day, they speak, night to night they reveal knowledge. There is no speech, no words, where their voice goes unheard. Their voice has gone out to all the earth and their words to the end of the world. In the heavens He pitched a tent for the sun. It is like a bridegroom coming out of his bridal chamber.

—Psalm 19:2-6, TLV

The Feasts of the Holy One are listed in order in the Book of Leviticus 23. Our Father's Holy Days are mentioned throughout the Bible, and they are all about Jesus. I like to refer to Jesus by His Hebrew name, Yeshua, which means salvation. One specific feast, The Feast of Trumpets, also called *A Day of Blowing*, is often described as the season of our Messiah's return. In the Book of Isaiah, the Holy One explains how He reckons time: "I declare the end from the beginning" (Isaiah 46:10, BSB). Meditate on the *end* being hidden in not only the Fall Feasts, but the Spring Feasts as well. The Holy One created the heavens and the earth in six days and then declared the 7th day His Sabbath rest at the end of His creation. This 7th day represents the longest day of rest, metaphorically, a 1,000 year reign with our Messiah when He returns. Hence, Adonai declared the end from the beginning. On the Feast of Trumpets, shofars are blown continually:

> *Adonai* spoke to Moses, saying: Speak to *Bnei-Yisrael* *[sons of Israel]*, saying: In the seventh month, on the first day of the month, you are to have a *Shabbat* rest, a memorial of blowing, a holy convocation.
>
> —Leviticus 23:23-24, TLV

Two silver trumpets were to be used to call the congregation to the tent of meeting and for having the camps set out (Numbers 10:1-10). The silver trumpets were to be blown by the High Priest or his representative. When the Messiah returns, we will hear the

Tekiah Gedolah (The Great Shofar). There are four sounds concerning this musical instrument:

- Tekiah: One long blast, a wake-up.

- Shevarim: Three medium blasts.

- Teruah: Nine blasts ending with a long blast.

- Tekiah Gedolah: One long forceful blast.

The Tekiah *Gedolah* meaning *great* is like the Tekiah but with a blast that brings power. In Matthew 24, this sound is called a "Great Shofar." Some translations say a loud trumpet call. The shofar is a trumpet—an ancient instrument:

> Then the sign of the Son of Man will appear in heaven, and then all the tribes of the land will mourn, and they will see the Son of Man coming on the clouds of heaven with power and great glory. He will send out His angels with a great *shofar*, and they will gather together His chosen from the four winds, from one end of heaven to the other.
>
> —Matthew 24:30-31, TLV

It is currently 2024, but during the season of 2015, I heard a shofar blowing loudly. I told my husband about the incident as he was out of town, and I pondered it in my heart. At that time, we lived in the middle of the woods, far away from anyone. The sound of it was so loud it resonated in my soul. I wondered what it could mean. Later, I discovered that there were others who had heard the sound of the shofar blast. This trumpet herald made world news. The shofar or trumpet blast sounds were named *"strange sounds from the sky"* and *"apocalyptic blast."* These noises were heard in places such as America, Canada, Germany, Hungary, Denmark, Sweden, England, Ukraine, and France. You can listen to these "Strange Sounds in the sky" on YouTube. Many scientists have tried to explain the reasoning behind the noise. One suggestion was that it could have been the shifting of tectonic plates. Still, I believe all these similarities and messages were being spoken to prepare the Body of Messiah for the coming days. Today, the labor pains mentioned in Matthew 24 by Yeshua are becoming harder as wars and great darkness fill the earth. God's people are told to not be alarmed:

> You will hear of wars and rumors of wars but see to it that you are not alarmed. These things must happen, but the end is still to come. Nation will rise against nation, and kingdom against kingdom. There will be famines and earthquakes in various places. All these are the beginning of birth pains.

> —Matthew 24:6-8, BSB

Much of Matthew 24 came to pass in 70 A.D. The Romans invaded Judea and this war lasted over three years. (See Flavius Josephus, *The Wars of the Jews; 67 A.D.-70 A.D)*. The Romans marched all over Judea, Samaria, Perea, Galilee, and the Negev, leaving paths of destruction and death. Back then they had no

CNN or Fox News Channels, but word of mouth, rumors, and reports of the invasion went forth to the surrounding areas. God's people were enslaved, killed, sent to do slave labor.

Yeshua warned the disciples to flee Judea because the whole land would be under siege not just Jerusalem, and their beloved Temple would be set ablaze in 70 A.D.

Jewish Virtual Library states:

> It is estimated that as many as one million Jews died in the Great Revolt against Rome. When people today speak of the almost two-thousand-year span of Jewish homelessness and exile, they are dating it from the failure of the revolt and the destruction of the Temple. Indeed, the Great Revolt of 66-70, followed some sixty years later by the Bar Kokhba revolt, were the greatest calamities in Jewish history prior to the Holocaust. [1]

Yeshua, the greatest prophet to ever walk the earth warns us of things to come and explains that when we see troubling events occurring on the earth, we will have an understanding that He is at the door. The Messiah tells us to have our bridal gowns prepared and our lamps burning. By keeping the Father's feasts days, we learn the season of His return. The Bible explains clearly that no man knows the day or the hour of the Messiah's return,

---

[1] https://www.jewishvirtuallibrary.org/the-great-revolt-66-70-ce

not even the Son, but only His Father. However, we can know the seasons, and the prophets of old can help prepare us for what lies ahead. Remember, history repeats itself.

How can we keep the Holy One's feasts today with clean hands and a pure heart? Are these ancient feasts for Christians today? These books, *Unveiling The Messiah In The Spring Feasts* and *Unveiling The Messiah In The Fall Feasts* bring unpretentious refinement and knowledge concerning the last days referred to as Jacob's trouble. It is my heart's desire that as you journey into the Messianic Kingdom and the Holy One's seasons that your spirit will be revived and renewed.

Feast of

Trumpets

Or

Yom Teruah

Chapter 1

The Feast of Trumpets or Yom Teruah

Part 1

The Feast of Trumpets is the fifth feast of Israel, and one that seems to have been hidden on purpose. Just as the Son said, "No one knows about that day or hour, not even the angels in heaven, nor the Son, but only the Father" (Matthew 24:36, BSB). Yeshua used a phrase his people would have been familiar with, " But of that day and hour no man knows." When the people heard those words, they would immediately have made the association with the Feast of Trumpets. There is only one feast day that begins at the New Moon and that is the Feast of Trumpets. The beginning of the 7th month on the Hebrew calendar is Tishrei 1. The name Tishri is not used in the Bible as it is a Babylonian name. Tishrei usually occurs in September–October on the Gregorian calendar.

Although, the Feast of Trumpets is not listed by name in the Bible. It lies in the shadows unless one is searching for it or enlightened to it. This feast is known to Christians as the Feast

1

of Trumpets but is called *Yom Teruah* in Hebrew. "The word Teruah is Strong's Concordance 8643, and it means a shout or blast of war, alarm, or joy." An old hymn *When the Roll is Called up Yonder, I'll be There* speaks of this day of blowing:

> *When the trumpet of the Lord shall sound and time shall be no more,*
>
> *And the morning breaks, eternal, bright and fair;*
>
> *When the saved of earth shall gather over on the other shore,*
>
> *And the roll is called up yonder, I'll be there.*

The Bible speaks of this day repeatedly:

> And He will send out His angels with a loud trumpet call, and they will gather His elect from the four winds, from one end of the heavens to the other.
>
> —Matthew 24:31, BSB

> For the Lord himself will come down from heaven with a rousing cry, with a call from one of the ruling angels, and with God's *shofar*; those who died united with the Messiah will be the first to rise.
>
> —I Thessalonians 4:16, CJB

In modern Judaism, it is called *Rosh Hashanah* or head of the year. However, there are four Jewish New Years on the Hebraic calendar. Do not be confused by this. Rosh Hashanah is the civil new year. The Feast of Trumpets begins a ten-day period leading up to the holiest day of the year, the Day of Atonement, which will be covered in a following chapter. The days between are called the Days of Awe and are filled with much introspection, reflection, and preparing one's heart. This is the one day of the year when our name is said to be sealed in the Book of Life. This represents the judgment seat of Messiah.

In ancient Israel, the people were on a lunar calendar controlled by the moon cycles. "'In the seventh month, on the first day of the month, you are to have a holy convocation; do not do any kind of ordinary work; it is a day of blowing the shofar for you" (Numbers 29:1, CJB). Every month there was a blowing of shofars according to Numbers Chapter 10, but the 5th feast, *Yom Teruah,* is a day of Shofar blast going forth like no other!

Today the majority of the world follows a solar calendar of 365.25 days per year. However, to go back to the 7th century and long before, all calendars were only 360-day years comprising of 12 months of exactly 30 days. The Hebrew word *Chodesh* is Strong's Concordance #2320, and it is derived from the root meaning *new, renewed,* and it is the origin of the word month. The Crescent New Moon is called *Chodesh* because it is the first time the moon is seen anew after being concealed in darkness. The moon is born again. We are born again.

In ancient times, there were new moon spotters in Israel who watched the sky until they saw the thin crescent declaring that a new month had begun. The new moon might occur 29.5 days after the last one or thirty days. The Book of Matthew hints to this watching for the return and being dressed and ready to meet the Messiah.

> Originally, the New Moon was not fixed by astronomical calculation but was solemnly proclaimed after witnesses had testified to the reappearance of the crescent of the moon (*Encyclopedia Judaica*, Vol. 12, p. 1039).

Again, the Bible tells us that Yeshua will send His angels with a LOUD trumpet blast in (Matthew 24:31). The same passage explains that there will appear a sign in the heavens. This Feast is the day we wait for. The Feast of Trumpets is the feast Christians refer to as the "rapture" of the Church. This trumpet blast is spoken of throughout scripture, and I must warn you it is a dark day for those unprepared:

> Woe to you who want the day of Adonai! Why do you want it, this Day of Adonai? It is darkness, not light; as if someone were to run from a lion, just to meet a bear; as if he entered a house, put his hand on the wall, just to be bitten by a snake. Won't the Day of Adonai be darkness, not light, completely dark, with no brightness at all?
>
> —Amos 5:18-20, CJB

The Book of Joel confirms the prophet Amos above as well as the Book of Zephaniah:

Near is the great day of the Lord, near and coming very quickly; Listen, the day of the Lord! In it, the warrior cries out bitterly. A day of wrath is that day, A day of trouble and distress, A day of destruction and desolation, A day of darkness and gloom, A daylight of thick clouds and darkness, A day of trumpet and battle cry against the fortified cities and the high corners towers.

—Zephaniah 1:14-16, NASB

As mentioned by the prophets of old, these holy days concern tribulation and judgment. We see this darkness today as wars, pestilence, murders, sex trafficking, drugs, earthquakes, tornados, floods, famine, and all kinds of woes that are happening upon the earth. However, amid this darkness, we also see people waking up and seeing passages in their Bibles they've never seen before. More Christians are worshiping the Holy One in Spirit and Truth as the Messiah proclaimed He was seeking such worshippers in John 4. Yeshua is looking for those with this type of heart. The Book of I Thessalonians gives us a glimpse of the Feast of Trumpets and shows us how we can be ready:

For you yourselves know full well that the day of the Lord will come just like a thief in the night. While they are saying "Peace and safety!" Then destruction will come upon them suddenly like labor pains upon a woman with child, and they will not escape. But you, brethren, are not in darkness, that the day would overtake you like a thief;

for you are all sons of light and sons of day. We are not of night nor of darkness; so then let us not sleep as others do, but let us be alert and sober.

—I Thessalonians 5:2-6, NASB

The reason Paul states these people are not in darkness is because His feasts, or *Moedim* in Hebrew, fall at His appointed times. On the Feast of Trumpets, our Messiah will return to get His Bride. We long for the Messiah to come set up His Kingdom and our millennial reign — the everlasting kingdom of Messiah Yeshua.

The Feast of Trumpets is a Jewish New Year, and instead of drunkenness and Time Square parties, it is a day celebrating the birthday of creation when Adonai said, "Let there be light." On the 1st of Nisan, the reign of kings was counted. If a king began to reign before, he still would not be counted until Nisan 1st. We too wait for our King Yeshua Messiah. Paul gives a thorough explanation in the Book of I Corinthians that concerns this glorious day of shofar blasts:

Behold, I tell you a mystery:

We shall not all sleep, but we shall all be changed — in a moment, in the twinkling of an eye, at the last *shofar*. For the *shofar* will sound, and the dead will be raised incorruptible, and we will be changed. For this corruptible must put on incorruptibility, and this mortal must put on immortality. But when this corruptible will have put on incorruptibility and this mortal will have put on immortality, then shall come to pass the saying that is written: "Death is swallowed up in victory." "Where, O Death, is your victory? Where, O Death, is your sting?"

—I Corinthians 15:51-55, TLV

The apostle called it the "last shofar." Not only did Paul expound on the Feast of Trumpets, so did Yeshua the Messiah:

And then the sign of the Son of Adam shall appear in the heaven, and then all the tribes of the earth shall mourn, and they shall see the Son of Adam coming on the clouds of the heaven with power and much esteem. "And He shall send His messengers with a great sound of a trumpet, and they shall gather together His chosen ones from the four winds, from one end of the heavens to the other."'

—Matthew 24:30-31, ISR

The signs have always been in the heavens. The wise men followed the signs. The Father told Abraham to look at the stars and to number them. Adonai was saying, "Look, Abraham, a nation is coming through your blood that will bring about the Messiah. The story of salvation is written in the stars. The twelve constellations are called the *Mazzaroth* in Hebrew. Each of the constellations showcase the whole Biblical story. The picture of Virgo features a woman with a stock of wheat in her left hand and a branch in her right hand. The brightest star in the constellation is located in the seed of the wheat. The star is called *Spica*, a Latin word meaning the branch.

EarthSky Website hosted by editor-in-chief, Deborah Byrd who also hosted the award-winning radio series EarthSky: A Clear Voice for Science. Byrd has an article, *Spica, the bright beacon of Virgo, is 2 Stars* that explains more of the metaphor which you may see. Virgo does not just represent the virgin Mary or Miriam but also Israel and we who have been engrafted into the olive tree:

> The star Spica – aka Alpha Virginis – is the brightest star in the constellation Virgo the Maiden. From a distance of about 250 light-years away, Spica appears to us on Earth as a lone bluish-white star in a quiet region of the sky. But Spica consists of two stars and maybe more. In fact, the pair are both larger and hotter than our sun, and they're separated by only 11 million miles (less than 18 million km). Plus, they orbit their common center of gravity in only four days. And the two stars in the Spica system are individually indistinguishable from a single point of light, even with a telescope. Only the analysis of its light with a spectroscope – an instrument that splits light into its component colors–revealed the dual nature of this star. [2]

---

[2] Spica, the bright beacon of Virgo, is 2 stars (earthsky.org)

The branch in the hand of Virgo is holding the Seed of Abraham in the right hand. Our Savior is called *by the prophet* Zechariah the *"Branch."*

Going further, there are 12 months, 12 zodiac signs, 12 apostles, 12 disciples, and 12 tribes of Israel. The sun is the light of the world. The Son/Yeshua is the light of the world—our risen Savior. The sun comes in the clouds and every eye sees the sun. The Son on Yom Teruah, Feast of Trumpets comes in the clouds and every eye will see Him!

> Behold, He is coming with the clouds, and every eye will see Him—even those who pierced Him. And all the tribes of the earth will mourn because of Him. So shall it be! Amen.
>
> —Revelation 1:7, BSB

The Heavens declare the glory of God. Psalms 19 tells us that the heavens have a Voice:

> The heavens declare the glory of God; the skies proclaim the work of His hands. Day after day they pour forth speech; night after night they reveal knowledge. Without speech or language, without a sound to be heard, their voice has gone out into all the earth, their words to the ends of the world. In the heavens He has pitched a tent for the sun [Son]. Like a bridegroom emerging from his chamber, like a champion rejoicing to run his course, it

rises at one end of the heavens and runs its circuit to the other; nothing is deprived of its warmth.

—Psalm 19:1-6, BSB

The constellations continue to speak: "And He said to them, 'Behold, of you having entered into the city, a man carrying a pitcher of water will meet you. Follow him into the house into which he enters.'" (Luke 22:10). The next house? The constellation Aquarius, she is a woman with a water pitcher. The Hebrew word for Spirit, ruach, is in nearly all cases feminine. Follow the Ruach, the Holy Spirit that soon will be poured out in Acts 2, the Day of Shavuot/Pentecost.

On the last and greatest day of the feast, Jesus stood up and called out in a loud voice, "If anyone is thirsty, let him come to Me and drink. Whoever believes in Me, as the Scripture has said: 'Streams of living water will flow from within him.' " He was speaking about the Spirit, whom those who believed in Him were later to receive. For the Spirit had not yet been given, because Jesus had not yet been glorified.

—John 7:37-39, BSB

What happens on Earth is happening in the heavens! I am not seeking the zodiac for an astrology reading of a horoscope. I am trying to reveal the heavens and the Earth to you because they mirror one other like the Tabernacle in the wilderness.

The following comes from *Felleskap for Fremtiden,* blog titled *The Mazzaroth in Bible prophecy:*

Revelation 1

And I turned to see (in the Heavenly scroll) the voice that spoke with me (Yahovah had spoken, identified himself as Aleph/Tav, the Father). And having turned I saw (in the Heavenly scroll) a golden lampstand (7) seven classical planets also seen as the seals over the Heavenly Scroll/stars) One like the Son of Man *(the constellation Orion represents the Son of Man in the Heavenly Scroll)* clothed with a garment (of the high Priest) down to the feet (tallit – Psalms 119:3) with a girdle of gold about His chest (chest plate of the High Priest Zachariah Chapter 3) The hair of his head was white like wool (John begins describing the constellation Orion, as white as snow, and his eyes were as a flame of fire, and his feet glowed like bronze which had been fired in a furnace, and His voice sounded like many waters (reference to the water-bearer Aquarius). And in his (Orion's') right hand he had seven stars (Orion looks like he is holding the remarkable 7 star cluster of the Pleiades) , and out of His mouth went a sharp, two-edged sword (the sword of Orion, a metaphor of the Word of Yahovah), and His face was like the sun (the sun is a metaphor of the Messiah) shining in its strength.

Also, Daniel compares our salvation and discipleship to the Heavens:

> Those who have insight will shine brightly like the brightness of the expanse of heaven, and those who lead the many to righteousness, like the stars forever and ever.

> —Daniel 12:3, NASB

Not only do we read about the "sign of the Son of man" in the Gospels, but we hear the phrase **"twinkling of an eye,"** and **"Thief in the night."** Both these phrases are Jewish idioms for the Feast of Trumpets. The trumpet is blown on several of these feasts, but on this one, it is a BLAST. This blast is mentioned in Revelation:

> The seventh angel sounded his trumpet, and there were loud voices in heaven, which said: The kingdom of the world has become the kingdom of our Lord and of his Messiah, and he will reign for ever and ever." And the twenty-four elders, who were seated on their thrones before God, fell on their faces and worshiped God, saying: "We give thanks to you, Lord God Almighty, the One who is and who was, because you have taken your great power and have begun to reign. The nations were angry, and your wrath has come. The time has come for judging the dead, and for rewarding your servants the prophets and

your people who revere your name, both great and small—
and for destroying those who destroy the earth.

—Revelation 11:15-18, NASB

In John 7 Yeshua shows up late to the Feast of Sukkot, we
see something similar written, but it offers a great warning:

> Now the bridegroom was late, so they all went to sleep. It
> was the middle of the night when the cry rang out, 'The
> bridegroom is here! Go out to meet him!' The girls all
> woke up and prepared their lamps for lighting. The foolish
> ones said to the sensible ones, "Give us some of your oil,
> because our lamps are going out." "No," they replied,
> "there may not be enough for both you and us. Go to the
> oil dealers and buy some for yourselves." But as they were
> going off to buy, the bridegroom came. Those who were
> ready went with him to the wedding feast, and the door
> was shut. Later, the other bridesmaids came. "Sir! Sir!"
> they cried, "Let us in!" But he answered, "Indeed! I tell
> you, I don't know you!" So stay alert, because you know
> neither the day nor the hour.

—Matthew 25:5-13, CJB

In Matthew 25, the bridegroom was late. This type of
mystery is recorded in the book of John. Yeshua's' brothers ask
him to go up to the Feast of Sukkot (tabernacles) with them and

show everyone His works and power to heal the sick and open the blind eyes. He answers them and with a clue to how He came to fulfil the Spring feasts, but the time for His fulfillment of the Fall feasts is not yet:

> "You, go on up to the festival; as for me, I am not going up to this festival now, because the right time for me has not yet come." Having said this, he stayed on in the Galil. But after his brothers had gone up to the festival, he too went up, not publicly but in secret. At the festival, the Judeans were looking for him. "Where is he?" they asked.
>
> —John 7:8-11, CJB

Yeshua tells his siblings that he isn't going to the festival because it's not His time, yet He does go. He starts off arriving in secret but eventually starts to teach. In John 2, Yeshua says something similar when the wedding supper ran out of wine and his mother approached Him:

> When the wine ran out, Jesus' mother said to Him, "They have no more wine." "Woman, why does this concern us?" Jesus replied. "My hour has not yet come.'"
>
> John 2:3-4, BSB.

John 2 happens around Passover, and John 7 happens around Sukkot; both involve time. Where is He? Why has He not returned as He promised? When will we be drinking from the cup of wine with Him? Peter warned that men during the last days would mock the day of our Messiah's return:

> Know this first of all, that in the last days mockers will come with their mocking, following after their own lusts, and saying, "Where is the promise of His coming? For ever since the fathers fell asleep, all continues just as it was from the beginning of creation." For when they maintain this, it escapes their notice that by the word of God the heavens existed long ago and the earth was formed out of water and by water, through which the world at that time was destroyed, being flooded with water. But by His word the present heavens and earth are being reserved for fire, kept for the Day of Judgment and destruction of ungodly men.
>
> —II Peter 3:3-7, NASB

The Bible says that there will be a people who will not be caught off guard when He returns. Also, Yeshua has returned now for over 2,000 years and His Feet have stood on the Mount of Olives. The wise can calculate the seasons, again as referenced in I Thessalonians:

> For you, yourselves know full well that the day of the Lord will come just like a thief in the night. While they are saying, "Peace and safety!" then destruction will come upon them suddenly like labor pains upon a woman with

child, and they will not escape. But you, brethren, are not in darkness, that the day would overtake you like a thief; for you are all sons of light and sons of day.

—I Thessalonians 5:2-4, NASB

Let us be children of the LIGHT.

Before we move to the next feast, the following chapter is an in-depth prophetic look at this shofar blast and the Feast of Trumpets concerning the year of release. Jubilee is the 50th year following seven cycles of seven years (*Shmita*).

The Feast of Trumpets or Yom Teruah

Part 2

Yeshua stood up in the synagogue and read a scroll from Isaiah 61 on the Sabbath day from the prophets. And the Bible says that when Yeshua had opened the scroll from the prophet Isaiah, He found the place where it was written:

> The Spirit of the Lord is upon me, because he hath anointed me to preach the gospel to the poor; he hath sent me to heal the brokenhearted, to preach deliverance to the captives, and recovering of sight to the blind, to set at liberty them that are bruised, to preach the acceptable year of the Lord. And he closed the book, and he gave it again to the minister and sat down. And the eyes of all them that were in the synagogue were fastened on him. And he began to say unto them, this day is this scripture fulfilled in your ears.
>
> —Luke 4:18-21 KJB

Yeshua was telling the people He is Jubilee. Yeshua came to open the eyes of both the physically and spiritually blind. He came to set those captive free from bondage and especially from the

19

corrupt leadership. Remember, the Book of John tells us that Yeshua is the Word, because He is full of wisdom and understanding. Yeshua read part of the proclamation from the Book of Isaiah 61, but He did not finish the whole declaration. Why would Yeshua stop speaking in the middle of a sentence? Yeshua left off verse 2: "To proclaim the acceptable year of the Lord, and the Day of Vengeance of our God" (Isaiah 61:2, NKJ). Yeshua came first as a Lamb. In Revelation5 we read of the Lion and the Lamb. We read of the symbol given to the tribe of Judah, a lion (Genesis 49:9), but after this is spoken, John sees not a lion but a lamb that was slain:

> Then one of the elders said to me, "Do not weep! Behold, the Lion of the tribe of Judah, the Root of David, has triumphed to open the scroll and its seven seals."
>
> Then I saw a Lamb who appeared to have been slain, standing in the center of the throne, encircled by the four living creatures and the elders. The Lamb had seven horns and seven eyes, which represent the seven Spirits of God sent out into all the earth. And He came and took the scroll from the right hand of the One seated on the throne.
>
> —Revelation 5:5-7, BSB

Yeshua comes as a Lamb with the seven spirits of God. The Spirit of the Lord, the Spirit of wisdom and understanding, the Spirit of counsel and strength, the Spirit of knowledge and the fear of the LORD. The Bible does not mention a lion laying down with a lamb, but a wolf. Isaiah 11 states, "And the wolf will dwell with the lamb" (Isaiah 11:6, NASB). Who is the wolf? We are told, "Benjamin is a ravenous wolf" (Genesis 49:27, BSB). A male lamb was offered up on the altar in Jerusalem each morning and evening (Exodus 29:38-42). The apostle Paul referred to Yeshua as "our Passover lamb." John the Baptist/Immerser said, Behold the Lamb of God who takes away the sins of the world." While reading the list below, picture each wolf surrendering to the Lamb of Yahweh:

1. Wolves: Wolves in sheep's clothing (Acts 20:29, Matthew 7:15-20)
2. "Her princes in her midst are like wolves tearing the prey, shedding blood, destroying lives to get dishonest gain" (Ezekiel 22:27, ESV)
3. "Her officials within her are roaring lions; her judges are evening wolves that leave nothing till the morning" (Zephaniah 3:3, ESV).

The Father has an order for everything, and He uses numbers and signs. He created the earth in six days and rested on the seventh and blessed it. The word *seven, Sabbath,* and *rest* mean the same thing. The Jubilee year is the year at the end of seven cycles of *Shmita* (seven). What does *Shmita* mean? The Hebrew people count and observe seven-year cycles. Every cycle would fulfill a Sabbatical year known as a *Shemitah* or *Shmita.* This word means to release—to be set free!

During Jubilee, slaves and prisoners were set free, debts were paid, and the land was given back to its rightful owner. One of the Ten Words/Ten Commandments talks about a Sabbath day of rest to keep holy and set apart, but the 50th Jubilee rest is over and above all. Restoration means to restore something back to its former condition. Think Garden of Eden before man sinned. In our world today, there is little rest. The earth is crying out. The world has watched in horror as wars and rumors of wars continue. Corruption in government leaders is off the charts. Another alarm is viruses spreading rapidly and toxic vaccines. Sickness and disease are on the rise. Racial tensions fill our streets; senseless killings, violence, and riots are on the rise:

> Nation will rise against nation and kingdom against kingdom (wars and rumors of wars), and there will be great earthquakes, and in various places plagues and famines; and there will be terrors and great signs from heaven.

> —Luke 21:10, ESV

On day six, God created man in His image and set him over the earth and told him to be fruitful, multiply, and subdue the earth and rule over every living creature. "Then God said, "Behold, I have given you every plant yielding seed that is on the surface of all the earth, and every tree which has fruit yielding seed; it shall be food for you; (Genesis 1:29, NASB). That's not Taco Bell or McDonald's. The food we eat today is mostly dead, and the seeds created by Monsanto cannot even reproduce because they have no life in them. Monsanto created Agent Orange, a deadly poison and also Round-Up, a weedkiller. Now they make seeds, dead seeds. They produce corn that humans cannot ingest and feed this corn to our cattle, chickens, and other animals we eat. Some blame cancer and other diseases on Satan, but men who are full of greed and do not care for the earth or even their future grandchildren, pollute and take from the earth and the sea without allowing it to rest. For more on Satan, pick up a copy of *Satan Unmasked.*

If we would leave the sea creatures alone, creatures that were designed by the Creator to clean the sea, we would have clear water. Author Susan Patterson of *Off the Grid News* explains why God would have never changed His food laws and how His ways protect us in her article, *God's Dietary Laws: Why Pigs, Crabs And Lobsters Are Bad For You:*

> Shellfish is a multi-billion-dollar business and eating such aquatic life is considered a delicacy in most parts of the world. We know that everything God created has a purpose; so what is the purpose of shellfish, then? Patterson explains how Science reveals what may have been God's reasons for declaring certain sea creatures unfit for human consumption. Unclean sea life consists of predatory scavengers known as bottom dwellers. These

23

fish and sea life that clean the ocean are full of toxins and can be harmful to human health. [3]

Patterson continues to explain why dietary laws were set up and need to be relooked at:

> Lobsters are nocturnal bottom walkers and scavengers that scavenge for dead animals and debris on the ocean floor – they are like the vultures of the oceans. Lobsters have even been seen burying dead fish and digging them up a little at a time to eat. Crabs will eat just about anything and are known as professional garbage hunters. According to the FDA, raw oysters, mussels, and clams are responsible for 85 percent of all illnesses caused by eating seafood. Such conditions as hepatitis A, salmonella, Norwalk virus, cholera, and paralytic shellfish poisoning are just a few of the problems that are often linked to shellfish consumption. [4]

Why would God suddenly change the design of the animals He created to clean up the earth? They were never designed as food, and if we would stop consuming them, they would do their job sweeping and cleansing the waters:

---

[3] https://www.offthegridnews.com/off-grid-foods/gods-dietary-laws-why-pigs-crabs-and-lobsters-are-bad-for-you/

[4] God's Dietary Laws: Why Pigs, Crabs And Lobsters Are Bad For You - Off The Grid News

From all that are in the waters, you may eat whatever has fins and scales, within the waters, in the seas and in the rivers. Those you may eat. [10] But any that do not have fins and scales in the seas or the rivers, among those that swarm on the waters, or among any of the living creatures that are in the waters, they are loathsome to you. [11] They are to be detestable to you. You shall not eat meat from them and you should detest their carcasses. [12] Whatever has neither fins nor scales in the waters, that is a detestable thing to you.

—Leviticus 11:9-12, TLV

Now that we have disobeyed the Father and feasted on swine and other animals and sea creatures that were never designed to be eaten but were designed to cleanse the earth, we have partaken of death. Aran Shaunak of *Food Unfolded* describes what is called a dead zone in the Gulf of Mexico in his article, *Cleaning The Seas with Mussel and Oyster Farms:*

Human activities – such as using nitrogen and phosphorous-rich fertilizers on land-based farms – have leeched huge amounts of these two nutrients into many coastal waters, with devastating results: the Gulf of Mexico, for example, now features a yearly summer "dead zone" of over 5,000 square miles in which there's too little oxygen for plants and fish to survive. [5]

Vertical ocean farms help reverse some of that harm. Shellfish, and mussels in particular, are excellent at pulling excess nitrogen and phosphorus out of the water around them.

What am I talking about? Dead things.

There was an older television series called *"The Walking Dead."* That's what we see now in the spirit and the natural—walking zombies. The dead seeds remind me of the food that has been fed to the assemblies, the Body of Yeshua in this late hour. That food is missing the truth, and further it is often poisoned with pride, prosperity, and ease. In the natural, our soil is not replenished with what it needs: vitamins, nutrients, copper, zinc, and iron, and in the spirit, our soul is not lit with the searing truth of Adonai's Word. We have walking dead people. Amos said:

> Behold, days are coming," declares the Lord GOD, "When I will send a famine on the land, not a famine for bread or a thirst for water, but rather for hearing the words of the LORD.

> —Amos 8:11, NASB

---

[5] Cleaning The Seas with Mussel and Oyster Farms (foodunfolded.com)

Our Father commanded us to let the land rest in the seventh year. The Holy One warned us about Everything happening to our planet and our water sources. He has an order for His creation, and God gave us instructions to take care of this earth and our temples, but we have failed miserably. Why? Greed. The Israelites were held in captivity in Babylon for seventy years because of the Sabbaths they did not keep. How should the Sabbath be kept? Not with heavy burdens no one can bear. This thing called "rest" affects Everything. The Dust Bowl is one proof of that, with causes stemming from over-plowed and over-grazed land. When we allow things to rest, they thrive. One reason God exiled His people was due to the land not being allowed to rest for eight complete Jubilee cycles plus part of a ninth. This was four hundred and ninety years, or seven Sabbatical years when God's people did not obey His commandment regarding the Sabbath year of rest. They were punished for it. The Holy One spoke through the prophet Jeremiah and told them:

> When seventy years have been completed for Babylon, I will visit you and fulfill my good word to you, to bring you back to this place. "For I know the plans that I have for you," declares the Lord, "plans for welfare and not for calamity to give you a future and a hope."
>
> —Jeremiah 29:10-11, NASB

The first portion of Jeremiah 29 is often used as a comforting verse full of promise, but this promise did not come about until God's people spent 70 years in Babylon. The prophet Daniel had been keeping track of this timeline, and in Chapter 9, Daniel knew that the seventy years would soon be ending. Daniel begins to fast, plead, and cry out for mercy on behalf of his people, Israel. Daniel could look at the prophets and form a timeline of when they would be returning to Israel.

The punishment for God's people was 70 years and had to do with rules for the land and the holy Sabbath. Adonai declared the Sabbath day as holy, set apart, blessed, and one that coincides with His patterns of seven (7) and His glorious return which is referred to metaphorically as a thousand-year day of rest. This 1,000-year reign is called the Feast of Tabernacles or Sukkot. The Sages state that this comes after the 6,000 years, day six of creation, and represents the 7,000th year. Some dispute a literal 1,000 years, but that is not my point here. My point is the seventh of seven feasts that occur in the seventh month for seven days (777):

> The LORD then spoke to Moses at Mount Sinai, saying, "Speak to the sons of Israel and say to them, 'When you come into the land which I shall give you, then the land shall have a sabbath to the LORD. Six years you shall sow your field, and six years you shall prune your vineyard and gather in its crop, but during the seventh year the land

shall have a sabbath rest, a sabbath to the LORD; you shall not sow your field nor prune your vineyard.'

—Leviticus 25:1-4, NASB

Adonai told them that in the sixth year He would give them so much they would not need to plow or reap the land: "Then I will so order My blessing for you in the sixth year that it will bring forth the crop for three years" (Leviticus 25:21, NASB):

> You shall count seven weeks of years, seven times seven years so that the time of the seven weeks of years shall give you forty-nine years. Then you shall sound the loud trumpet on the tenth day of the seventh month. On the Day of Atonement, you shall sound the trumpet throughout all your land. And you shall consecrate the fiftieth year, and proclaim liberty throughout the land to all its inhabitants.
>
> —Leviticus 25:8-10, ESV

During the Jubilee, the Holy One called His people to stop sowing and reaping and to rest in Him (Leviticus 25). Could Yeshua return in the year of Jubilee? Remember that's a day no man knows the hour except the Father, but we can be children of light and know when to be looking. "It shall be established for ever as the moon, and as a faithful witness in heaven" (Psalm 89:37, KJB). If we go by His calendar in the heavens, we will know the seasons. Everything was restored during the Jubilee. I believe "That Day" could possibly fall on a Jubilee year and the Feast Day. "That Day," could be also a symbol of our own personal salvation:

> Note, first of all, the prophetic words of Elijah: "Elijah told Judah 'the world will endure no less than 85 Jubilees, and on the last Jubilee the son of David will come'" (Talmud, sanh.97b). [6]

The rabbis have taught there will be a total of 120 Jubilee cycles (6000 years) from the time God created man until the beginning of the messianic kingdom here on earth. The Jewish book of Jubilees tells us that the 6,000 years of man's rule should not be counted from the date of creation, but implies that we should count from the date of Adam and Eve's transgression in the Garden of Eden: [7]

> For a thousand years in Your sight Are like yesterday when it passes by, Or as a watch in the night.
>
> —Psalm 90:4, NASB

According to the Bible, Yeshua will rule the earth for 1,000 years:

---

[6] http://www.come-and-hear.com/sanhedrin/sanhedrin_97.html

[7] https://www.breakingisraelnews.com/68859/the-mystery-of-the-lost-jubilee-part-xx-6000-years-old-opinion/

And I saw thrones, and they sat upon them, and judgment was given unto them; and I saw the souls of them that were beheaded for the witness of Jesus, and for the word of God, and which had not worshipped the beast, neither had received his mark upon their foreheads, or in their hands; and they lived and reigned with Christ a thousand years. But the rest of the dead lived not again until the thousand years were finished.

—Revelation 20:4-5, KJB

This "millennial rest" of one-thousand years is termed a "Sabbath rest" by the author of the Book of Hebrews:

Since, then, it remains for some to enter His rest, and since those who formerly heard the good news did not enter because of their disobedience, God again designated a certain day as "Today," when a long time later He spoke through David as was just stated: "Today, if you hear His voice, do not harden your hearts."

For if Joshua had given them rest, God would not have spoken later about another day. There remains, then, a Sabbath rest for the people of God. For whoever enters God's rest also rests from his own work, just as God did from His. Let us, therefore, make every effort to enter that rest, so that no one will fall by following the same pattern of disobedience.

—Hebrew 4:6-9, TLV

We wait for this glorious day and a Sabbath rest for God's people. Remember, we all can find rest now in Him and by the comfort of the Holy Spirit, but the Bible says that He fixed a particular day. This same Messiah arose from the dead, not necessarily on Sunday morning, but possibly on the Sabbath. There never was a "Good Friday" or "Easter Sunday sunrise service." In Luke 4, Yeshua from the tribe of Judah was giving the people a proclamation. He was telling them, He was Jubilee. He was fulfilling the beginning of Isaiah's prophecy. On Yeshua's return, He will fulfill the ending:

> . . . to proclaim the year of the LORD's favor and the day of our God's vengeance, to comfort all who mourn, to console the mourners in Zion—to give them a crown of beauty for ashes, the oil of joy for mourning, and a garment of praise for a spirit of despair. So they will be called oaks of righteousness, the planting of the LORD, that He may be glorified.

—Isaiah 61:2-3, BSB

The number of passages concerning the 7th day (Future Jubilee) is astounding. Before reading the following verses carefully, consider, did Yeshua/Jesus stop obeying His Father's

Word? Did He do away with keeping these cycles of seven? Did somehow, Yeshua from the tribe of Judah, suddenly become a Roman Catholic wearing a Roman robe and celebrating on the day of the sun god? During the time of the Roman empire, Julius Caesar was emperor. He transformed the calendar into a solar calendar. Although Constantine in 325 AD had a big part in changing the day of worship from Sabbath to Sunday, this shift started centuries earlier:

Justin's First Apology 67 (prior to his martyr in 165 AD):

And on the day called Sunday, all who live in cities or in the country gather together to one place, and the memoirs of the apostles or the writings of the prophets are read, as long as time permits; then, when the reader has ceased, the overseer verbally instructs, and exhorts to the imitation of these good things.

But Sunday is the day on which we all hold our common assembly, because it is the first day on which God, having wrought a change in the darkness and matter, made the world; and Jesus Christ our Saviour on the same day rose from the dead."

–Justin Martyr, *1 Apol. LXVII* in *Ante-Nicene Fathers: The Apostolic Fathers with Justin Martyr and*

Irenaeus, Vol. 1, Ed. A. Cleveland Coxe (Grand Rapids, MI: Eerdmans, 2001), 186. [8]

However, we read of 1st century Believers, including the apostles, still keeping the Sabbath in the New Testament:

1. And they went into Capernaum. Right away, on *Shabbat*, He (Yeshua) entered the synagogue and began to teach" (Mark 1:21, TLV).

2. "Then Jesus came to Nazareth, where He had been brought up. As was His custom, He entered the synagogue on the Sabbath. And when He stood up to read, the scroll of the prophet Isaiah was handed to Him" (Luke 4:16-17, BSB).

3. "One Sabbath Jesus was teaching in one of the synagogues" (Luke 13:10, BSB).

His Sabbaths are a sign between Him and Us:

4. "And the LORD said to Moses, "Tell the Israelites, 'Surely you must keep My Sabbaths, for this will be a sign between Me and you for the generations to come, so that you may know that I am the LORD who sanctifies you" (Exodus 31:13, BSB).

---

[8] "On the day called Sunday" by Justin Martyr (A.D. 110-165) - Tolle Lege

His Sabbath Day is one of the Ten Commandments:

> "Remember the Sabbath day, to keep it holy" (Exodus 20:8, NKJ).

5. "On the following Sabbath, nearly the whole city gathered to hear the word of the Lord" (Acts 13:44, BSB).

Paul the apostle explains in Acts 15, that the new converts will hear the Torah every Sabbath and learn more concerning the covenant they have been engrafted into:

6. It is my judgment, therefore, that we should not cause trouble for the Gentiles who are turning to God. Instead, we should write and tell them to abstain from food polluted by idols, from sexual immorality, from the meat of strangled animals, and from blood. For Moses has been proclaimed in every city from ancient times and is read in the synagogues on every Sabbath" (Acts 15:19-21, BSB). (No heavy burdens here)

7. "On the Sabbath we went outside the city gate along the river, where it was customary to find a place of prayer. After sitting down, we spoke to the women who had gathered there" (Acts 16:13, BSB).

8. As was his custom, Paul went into the synagogue, and on three Sabbaths he reasoned with them from the Scriptures, explaining and proving that the Christ had to suffer and rise from the dead. "This Jesus I am

proclaiming to you is the Christ," he declared. Some of the Jews were persuaded and joined Paul and Silas, along with a large number of God-fearing Greeks and quite a few leading women" (Acts 17:2-4, BSB).

9. "Every Sabbath he reasoned in the synagogue, trying to persuade Jews and Greeks alike" (Acts 18:4, BSB).

Whenever this topic is brought up, some will retort with, "Is not every day The Lord's Day?" Or "I worship God every day." Some will explain that Jesus arose from the grave on Sunday, making it The Lord's Day, but in *Unveiling the Messiah in the Spring Feasts*, I debunked this dogma. Although most of us were not raised as Jews or 1st century Believers, more than likely most of us attend or used to attend a Sunday morning congregation, that is not the point. Many are now celebrating the day of rest on Saturday. I am not judging anyone celebrating and resting on Sunday, or any other day, I am simply pointing out that the 7th day is when our Creator rested, and it is also the 4th commandment. Remember, Yeshua was often rebuking the leadership because they had made the Sabbath a burden and added many rules. Yeshua even explained to the religious leaders that His Father has work to do, and He, too, has work to do on the Sabbath. He was healing the sick, opening the eyes of the physically blind and the spiritually blind.

We were all raised to keep traditions, whether Christian or Jewish, or some other form of worship. Unveiling Messiah in the

Fall Feast will open your eyes to passages in your Bible you might have overlooked, teaching you the history and traditions of our Master, Yeshua Messiah.

The Day of

Atonement

or

Yom

HaKippurim

Chapter 2

The Day of Atonement or

Yom HaKippurim

Part 1

The Day of Atonement, also known as the Days of Repentance, are ten days. The days between the Feast of Trumpets and the Day of Atonement are called the Days of Awe or *Yamim Noraim* in Hebrew, meaning terrible days, Days of Awe, High Holidays. This represents the judgment. These ten days represent a more significant period to the Jewish audience, but we who know Messiah have been given the promise of redemption:

> We implore you on behalf of Christ: Be reconciled to God. God made Him who knew no sin to be sin on our behalf, so that in Him we might become the righteousness of God.
>
> —II Corinthians 5:20-21, BSB

My little children, I am writing these things to you so that you will not sin. But if anyone does sin, we have an advocate before the Father—Jesus Christ, the Righteous One. He Himself is the atoning sacrifice for our sins, and not only for ours but also for the sins of the whole world.

—I John 1:2, BSB

The Book of Hebrews lays out complete understanding of the Day of Atonement and the High Priest Yeshua, who offered himself once and for all. In this way, although many say the fall feasts have not happened yet and that we are waiting for them to unfold, we see Yeshua already offered himself:

After saying above, "Sacrifices and offerings and whole burnt offerings and sin offerings You did not desire, nor did You delight in them" (those which are offered according to *Torah*), then He said, "Behold, I come to do Your will." He takes away the first to establish the second. By His will we have been made holy through the offering of the body of Messiah *Yeshua* once for all.

Indeed, every *kohen* stands day by day serving and offering the same sacrifices again and again, which can never take away sins. But on the other hand, when this One offered for all time a single sacrifice for sins, He sat down at the right hand of God— waiting from then on, until His enemies are made a footstool for His feet. For by one offering He has perfected forever those being made holy.

—Hebrews 10:8-14, TLV

On Yom Kippur, we can celebrate because our sins have been atoned for once and for all by Yeshua, but that does not give us a license to sin. Nonetheless, according to Judaism, judgment is pronounced on Rosh Hashanah/Feast of Trumpets, but it is not complete or sealed until Yom Kippur (Day of Atonement). This seal of protection is written about in both the Old Testament and the New:

> The LORD said to him, "Go through the midst of the city, even through the midst of Jerusalem, and put a mark on the foreheads of the men who sigh and groan over all the abominations which are being committed in its midst." But to the others, He said in my hearing, "Go through the city after him and strike; do not let your eye have pity and do not spare."
>
> —Ezekiel 9:4-5, NASB

The mark was the Hebrew letter taw/tav. Tav is the last letter of the Hebrew Aleph-bet and means seal or mark. Yeshua said He was the beginning and the end. In the Book of Ezekiel, the men who were repenting and aware of all the sin surrounding them were marked, sealed, and covered in the day of slaughter. And again, in Revelation 7, and in other passages, we get confirmation on His set apart people being sealed:

> Do not harm the land or the sea or the trees until we seal the servants of our God *with a mark of ownership* on their foreheads.
>
> —Revelation 7:3, TLV

> And in Him, having heard and believed the word of truth—the gospel of your salvation—you were sealed with the promised Holy Spirit, who is the pledge of our inheritance until the redemption of those who are God's possession, to the praise of His glory.
>
> —Ephesians 1:13-14, BSB

> And do not grieve the Holy Spirit of God, in whom you were sealed for the day of redemption.
>
> —Ephesians 4:30, BSB

The passage from Revelation 7 is not the rapture: "The one who endures to the end, he will be saved" (Matthew 24:13, NASB). Christian theologians teach that we are airlifted, while the unrighteous are left behind. However, it is the righteous ones that are left behind, not the unrighteous. Stay with me, as we investigate each verse used to support the rapture doctrine. I know this goes against what many have been taught, but more information is available today:

There will be two women grinding at the same place; one will be taken, and the other will be left. "Two men will be in the field; one will be taken, and the other will be left." And answering they said to Him, "Where, Lord?" And He said to them, "Where the body is, there also the vultures will be gathered."

—Luke 17:35-37, NASB

Other translations such as the *King James Bible* replace vulture with eagles, which are also flesh-eating birds. "Wheresoever the body *is*, thither will the eagles be gathered together" (Luke 17:37, KJB). Where are these that are taken going? What location? This is what the disciples asked Yeshua. He answered and told them that the vultures would gather and eat their flesh. Whose flesh? The unrighteous— those who have a fleshly nature, but the Eagles/vultures will be eating their flesh. We can look at this in the natural or the spirit. Is this the Great Supper mentioned in Revelation? The Book of Revelation is an apocryphal book with deep metaphors, so much of the writings are mysterious:

Then I saw a single angel standing in the sun, and with a loud voice he cried out to all the birds flying high in the sky, "Come, gather for the great banquet of God— to eat the flesh of kings and the flesh of generals and the flesh of mighty men, the flesh of horses and those riding on them, the flesh of all men, both free and slave, both small and great!"

—Revelation 19:17-18, TLV

From the verses we have covered, clearly, we want to be left behind until a particular time, not taken. Yeshua in Luke 17 is quoting a portion from the Book of Job when he says, "Wheresoever the body *is*, thither will the eagles be gathered together:

> He [horse and rider] cannot stand still when the *shofar* sounds. At the blast of the *shofar*, he says, 'Aha!' From a distance he smells battle, the shout of the captains and the battle cry. "Is it by your wisdom that the hawk soars, spreading its wings toward the south? Is it by your command that an eagle soars and builds its nest high? It dwells on a cliff and spends the night there, on a rocky crag and stronghold. From there it searches for food; its eyes detect it from afar. Its young ones suck up blood, and where the slain are, there it is.
>
> —Job 39:25-30, TLV

The Book of Proverbs continues the thread of vultures and disobedience:

As for the eye that mocks a father and scorns obedience to a mother, may the ravens of the valley pluck it out and young vultures devour it.

—Proverbs 30:17, *BSB*

When reading Matthew 13, Yeshua presents a parable concerning the righteous and the unrighteous by using tares and wheat, and, again, we see the righteous are not the ones taken first. What are tares?

Matthew 13:24-30. Zizanium, [tares], is a kind of darnel, bastard wheat. This wheat known as darnel looks like real wheat, but the true wheat when it gets its fruit, bows its head lowly:

> Arabic, zowan, Hebrew zownin; zan means "nausea." Not our vetch *[genus Vicia, of the legume family]*, but darnel; at first impossible to distinguish from wheat or barley, until the wheat's ear is developed, when the thin fruitless ear of the darnel is detected. Its root so intertwines with that of the wheat that the farmer cannot separate them, without plucking up both, "till the time of harvest." The seed is like wheat, but smaller and black, and when mixed with wheat flour causes dizziness, intoxication, and paralysis; Lolium temulentum, "bearded darnel", the only deleterious grain among all the numerous grasses. [9]

---

[9] https://bible-history.com/faussets/t/tares/

Matthew 13 explains the wheat and the tares thoroughly:

> The kingdom of heaven is like a man who sowed good seed in his field. But while everyone was asleep, his enemy came and sowed weeds among the wheat, and slipped away. When the wheat sprouted and bore grain, then the weeds also appeared.
>
> The owner's servants came to him and said, "Sir, didn't you sow good seed in your field? Where then did the weeds come from?" "An enemy did this," he replied. So the servants asked him, "Do you want us to go and pull them up?" "No," he said, "if you pull the weeds now, you might uproot the wheat with them."
>
> Let both grow together until the harvest. At the proper time, I will tell the harvesters, "First collect the weeds and tie them in bundles to be burned; then gather the wheat into my barn."
>
> —Matthew 13:24-30, BSB

Those taken first are not the raptured people many Evangelists and pastors said were getting airlifted. Even when Yeshua prays to His Father in John Chapter 17, He says, "I do not ask You to take them out of the world, but to keep them from the evil one" (John 17:30, NASB).

Noah and his family were left behind; the unrighteous were taken. Lot and his daughters were left behind; the unrighteous were taken. The passages from Luke 17 and Matthew 24 have been twisted. Yeshua plainly said, "Wherever the corpse is, there the vultures will gather" (Matthew 24:28, ESV). One of the main passages used as a proof text for the rapture doctrine comes from I Thessalonians 4:

> For this we say to you by the word of the Lord, that we who are alive and remain until the coming of the Lord, will not precede those who have fallen asleep. For the Lord Himself will descend from heaven with a shout, with the voice of the archangel and with the trumpet of God, and the dead in Christ will rise first. Then we who are alive and remain will be caught up together with them in the clouds to meet the Lord in the air, and so we shall always be with the Lord.
>
> —I Thessalonians 4:15-17, NASB

Author and Hebrew scholar, Dr. Skip Moen offers answers to this perplexing verse concerning being caught up or seized on his website, Hebrew Word Study, *The "Rapture" Monkey Wrench:*

> The Greek word for "caught up" is *"harpazō"* and means "to seize, to carry off by force" or "to snatch away." There's just one little problem. *harpazō* is used idiomatically in literature during the time Paul wrote. The Book of Enoch and the documents from the Qumran community (Dead

Sea Scrolls) use the same Greek word, and the same imagery, to describe victory, not rapture. In fact, there are many Jewish apocalyptic texts that read like Paul's writings but have nothing to do with a physical rapture. [10]

Dr. Moen concludes his teaching by expressing why he is writing about the word *harpazo* and how the meaning of a word must be determined by the way the word is used in the culture of origin, not by the way later cultures think about the same word. Since Paul was part of the first century eschatological outlook, it is appropriate to ask, "What did the word mean to those who used it in the first century?"

Matthew 13 expresses the same momentous point—the unrighteous are removed first, and those who love Adonai being spared:

The harvest is the end of the age, and the reapers are angels. Therefore just as the weeds are gathered up and burned with fire, so shall it be at the end of the age. The Son of Man will send forth His angels, and they will gather out of His kingdom all stumbling blocks and those who practice lawlessness. They will throw them into the fiery furnace; in that place will be weeping and gnashing of

---

[10] The "Rapture" Monkey Wrench | Hebrew Word Study | Skip Moen

teeth. Then the righteous will shine forth as the sun in the kingdom of their Father. He who has ears, let him hear!

—Matthew 13:39-43. TLV

The harvest is at the end of days and the unrighteous tares are taken first. Christians, have we been lied to? The *rapture* is a hoax created by John Nelson Darby around 1830. *Biblical Eschatology* gives more insight as to how Darby may have come up with the idea of the rapture doctrine in an article titled *The History of the Rapture*. The article addresses Margaret MacDonald, a woman in 1830 who was part of a cult and claimed to have a prophetic vision that hinted to the rapture, but doctors believed her to be very ill. After MacDonald, Edward Irving picked up the rapture doctrine, and, after Irving, the Millerites. Regardless, the rapture doctrine is something fairly new, and it is not found anywhere between the pages of the Bible:

> In spite of Margaret's condition, people believed her. Not ministers trained in the Word, not those who were pious Christians, not those with discernment, but those seeking a new fad and emotional experience, just as so many do today. By the way, she was a cultist! Then another cult group in England picked this up by the name of "The Catholic Apostolic Church," headed by Edward Irving (1792-1834). After that, another cult group called the "Millerites" predicted the return of Christ on October 22,

49

1844. It did not happen; that should have been a clue, but this would not die.

At the same time, this belief was then picked up by Irish born minister, lawyer, evangelist and author, John N. Darby in 1930, who took this new fad to America in 1862 to 1877. He was looking for a "hook" in his motivational Bible speeches to attract crowds in England and on his visit to the Americas, USA, and Canada. [11]

Many theologians use a verse from I Thessalonians 4:17, that implies we will meet the Lord in the "air:"

Then we who are alive, who are left behind, will be caught up together with them in the clouds, to meet the Lord in the air—and so we shall always be with the Lord.

—I Thessalonians 4:17, TLV

This word *air* is the Greek word *aer* and has nothing to do with the stratosphere. "Strong's Greek #109: Air, the lower air we breathe. From *aemi*; *air*." [12] If we lean on "history repeating itself," we can look at the warnings both Yeshua and John gave to the people during that time period. Yeshua warned that not one stone would be left upon another concerning their temple.

---

[11] The History of the Rapture | Biblical Eschatology Blog

[12] https://biblehub.com/interlinear/1_thessalonians/4.htm

He was prophesying 70 AD. During John's time, there was much going on concerning tyrants and evil dictators.

The rapture doctrine causes many Christian believers to live at ease and not prepare for what is coming. It creates complacency and boasting of the worse kind. There is all manner of prideful talk of being airlifted and cars running off the road, airplanes crashing because the pilot was "airlifted" and the unrighteous on board were not. They laugh and explain they won't be here for any kind of tribulation, but that is not what Yeshua Messiah taught in Matthew 24. I would go further and state that tribulation was happening in World War I, World War II, and the Great Depression. Tribulation is here. Follow the order of what is happening as Yeshua lays out the unfolding of what will take place before His coming. This is also according to 70 AD:

1. Many will come in His Name, but they are antichrists.
2. There will be wars and rumors of wars.
3. Nation will rise against nation and kingdom against kingdom.
4. There will be earthquakes in various places.
5. They will hand you over to be persecuted and kill you.
6. You will be hated by all the nations because of My Name.
7. Many will fall away and will betray one another and hate one other.
8. Many false prophets will arise and lead many astray.

9. *Torahlessness*—lawlessness will multiply, the love of many will grow cold.

10. The Good News of the kingdom will be proclaimed in the whole world as a testimony to all the nations.

11. The abomination of desolation spoken of through Daniel the prophet will stand in the Holy Place.

12. Great trouble, such as has not happened since the beginning of the world.

13. False messiahs and false prophets will rise up and show great signs and wonders to lead people astray.

If people tell you Yeshua is in the wilderness, do not go out:

> For just as lightning comes from the east and flashes as far as the west, so also will be the coming of the Son of Man. For wherever the carcass is, there the vultures will gather.
>
> —Matthew 24:27-28, TLV

But immediately after the trouble of those days, "the sun will be darkened, and the moon will not give its light and the stars will fall from heaven and the powers of the heavens will be shaken. Then the sign of the Son of Man will appear in heaven, and then all the tribes of the land will mourn, and they will see 'the Son of Man coming on the clouds of heaven' with power and great glory. He will send out His angels with a great *shofar*, and they will gather together His chosen from the four winds, from one end of heaven to the other."

—Matthew 24:29-30, TLV

Yeshua does not speak of Believers skipping the days of darkness, the wars, the rumors of wars, or any of the tribulation until the end.

At the beginning of this topic concerning the rapture we looked at scriptures that showcased the wicked being taken first. They were described as tares that were bundled and thrown in the fire. When Yeshua's disciples inquired as to where those will be taken while working in the fields, He responded curiously by stating that where the eagles or vultures were gathered, there these people would be also. Could these eagles and vultures represent prophets and apostles and teachers of His Word? Their voices are as a fire that eats away the fleshly nature and causes men to repent:

> Then I saw an angel standing in the sun, and he cried out with a loud voice, saying to all the birds which fly in midheaven, "Come, assemble for the great supper of God, so that you may eat the flesh of kings and the flesh of commanders and the flesh of mighty men and the flesh of horses and of those who sit on them and the flesh of all men, both free men and slaves, and small and great."

—Revelation 19:17-18, NASB

How does one eat man's flesh? John said he came to preach repentance and baptism, but that Yeshua was coming to immerse us in fire. Fire gets the dross out of gold. The Day of Atonement is referred to as a "day of trouble or Jacob's trouble" by the Jewish people:

> Alas! For that day is great, so that none is like it: it is even the time of Jacob's trouble, but he shall be saved out of it.
>
> —Jeremiah 30:7, NASB

David wrote about this day, and so did many others:

> Blow a trumpet in Zion, And sound an alarm on My holy mountain! Let all the inhabitants of the land tremble, For the day of the LORD is coming; Surely it is near.
>
> —Joel 2:1, NASB

The Prophet Ezekiel wrote about it:

> For the day is near, Even the day of the LORD is near; It will be a day of clouds, A time of doom for the nations.
>
> —Ezekiel 30:3, NASB

Also Joel:

> Gather the people, sanctify the congregation, assemble the elders, gather the children and the nursing infants. Let the bridegroom come out of his room and the bride

out of her bridal chamber. Let the priests, the LORD'S ministers, Weep between the porch and the altar.

—Joel 2:16-17, NASB

King David knew about this place of protection:

For in the day of trouble He will conceal me in His tabernacle; in the secret place of His tent He will hide me; He will lift me up on a rock.

—Psalm 27:5, NASB

Yeshua said he was going away to prepare a bridal chamber for us. In the ancient Hebrew days, a wedding first started with the betrothal and time of courtship. While the man was working on the wedding chamber for his bride (John 14:2), he would wait until his father told him the house was complete, and then he would come for his bride. He would steal his bride away like a thief in the night, and then he would take her into his chamber for seven days. A day unto the Lord is but a thousand years and a thousand years a day (II Peter 3:8).

These ten days are called the *yomim nora'im* or Days of Awe in modern Judaism. During the Days of Awe, it is believed that Adonai seals our names, which He has written in a book called the Book of Life. If you want to learn more about these ten days, known as the Days of Awe in your Bible, you can find references in the seven churches listed in Revelation and the story of the ten virgins, five wise and five foolish (Matthew 25). There is one assembly which has ten days of testing, the assembly in Smyrna:

> And unto the angel of the church in Smyrna write; These things saith the first and the last, which was dead, and is alive; I know thy works, and tribulation and poverty, (but thou art rich) and I know the blasphemy of them which say they are Jews, and are not, but are the synagogue of Satan. Fear none of those things which thou shalt suffer behold, the devil shall cast some of you into prison, that ye may be tried; and ye shall have tribulation ten days: be thou faithful unto death, and I will give thee a crown of life. He that hath an ear, let him hear what the Spirit saith unto the churches; He that overcometh shall not be hurt of the second death.
>
> —Revelation 2:8-11, KJV

Yeshua tells the people to be faithful until death, until the end. The end of what? Jacobs's trouble or the Days of Awe. What is Jacob's trouble and where is this found in the Bible?

> These are the words that the LORD spoke concerning Israel and Judah. Yes, this is what the LORD says: "A cry of panic is heard—a cry of terror, not of peace. Ask now, and see: Can a male give birth? Why then do I see every man with his hands on his stomach like a woman in labor and every face turned pale? How awful that day will be!

None will be like it! **It is the time of Jacob's distress, but he will be saved out of it.**

—Jeremiah 30:4-7, BSB

We have been crucified with the Messiah and have been born anew. If we confess our sins, He is faithful to forgive us. If we are walking with the Holy One/Messiah daily, and we fall into sin, He will convict us to repent, make things right with our brothers and sisters, and continue on our journey. But what if we keep falling away? Hebrews 10 has a fearful word for this issue:

> For if we keep on sinning willfully after we have received the knowledge of the truth, there no longer remains a sacrifice for sins, but only a terrifying expectation of judgment and a fury of fire about to devour the enemies of God.
>
> For we know the One who said, "Vengeance is Mine; I will repay," and again, "*Adonai* will judge His people." It is a terrifying thing to fall into the hands of the living God.
>
> —Hebrews 10:26, 27, 30-31, TLV

In our next chapter we will follow all of Jacob's trouble and what this could possibly mean today.

The Day of Atonement or Yom HaKippurim

Jacob's Trouble

Part 2

The Bible mentions tribulation or a time of Jacob's Trouble. The Messiah states that tribulation will come upon the whole earth. In Matthew 24, after Yeshua mentions wars, floods, earthquakes, the sun darkening, and the heavens shaken, only after all those things are completed does the Messiah say we should look for Him:

> At that time the sign of the Son of Man will appear in heaven, and all the tribes of the earth will mourn. They will see the Son of Man coming on the clouds of heaven, with power and great glory.
>
> —Matthew 24:30, BSB

All the apostles went through tribulation. John confirms this in his prophecy that he is partnering with those who are in tribulation and preserving:

I, John, your brother and partner in the tribulation and kingdom and perseverance that are in Jesus, was on the island of Patmos because of the word of God and my testimony about Jesus.

—Revelation 1:9, BSB

In the Book of Jeremiah, the prophet compares what the patriarch Jacob went through to what God's people would go through due to their sins and rebellion, but also lets them know they will be saved out of it: "It is the time of Jacob's [trouble] distress, but he will be saved out of it" (Jeremiah 30:7, BSB). The Holy One was sending His people to Babylon as punishment. They would be in exile for 50-70 years. Author Thomas Williamson breaks down the different interpretations concerning the prophecy *"Time of Jacob's Trouble - Future or Fulfilled?"*

> In Jeremiah 29:1-4 the prophet says he is writing to the first group of captives who are already in Babylon. He assures them that God will take care of them and cause them to prosper (29:5-7). He says they will not be coming back to Judah immediately as promised by the false prophets, but that they will be restored from captivity after 70 years (29:8-14). In 29:15-32 Jeremiah rebukes various false prophets, some of whom will shortly be executed by the King of Babylon. His prophecies in chapter 30 are simply a continuation of chapter 29 - in

30:3 he promises again, as he did in 29:8-14, that the Jews will be returning to their homeland in Palestine. Jeremiah 30:18 speaks of the return of the captives and the rebuilding of Jerusalem which the Babylonians had left in a ruined state. There is absolutely no reason to believe that in 30:7, with the mention of the "time of Jacob's trouble," the prophet has suddenly jumped out of the context of events in the 6th Century BC, to refer to some mysterious, unknown crisis that is to come upon the Jews 2600 years later. [13]

However, prophecy, like history, can repeat itself. Can God's people go through more than one "Jacob's Trouble?" What could be worse than the Holocaust? Over six million Jews were murdered. Is the prophecy from Jeremiah already fulfilled? To understand the phrase "Jacob's trouble," we need to know Jacob's story and all his woes.

The story of Jacob begins in Genesis 25. Jacob had a twin brother named Esau. When his mother Rebecca is pregnant with the twins, she inquires to the Holy One for answers and receives a proclamation:

---

[13] http://biblicalexaminer.org/W_Jacob%27s%20Troubles.html

Two nations are in your womb, and two peoples from within you will be separated; one people will be stronger than the other, and the older will serve the younger.

—Genesis 25:23, BSB

Jacob is smooth, and Esau is hairy. Several scholars describe this as an example of our beastly, sinful nature. The mantra compares Jacob and Esau to our lower and higher selves striving against one another. We learn from the story in Genesis that Jacob was a man of tents, and Esau was a hunter. One day, Esau comes in from the field famished and asks for "that red stuff" and sells his birthright to Jacob for a bowl of lentils and acquires the name of a nation, Edom (red).

Continuing with Jacob and his troubles, we learn that not only does Jacob trick Esau out of the birthright, but Jacob DISGUISES himself as Esau. The following central plot in Jacob's story is reminiscent of *Little Red Riding Hood and the Big Bad Wolf.* Jacob's mother overhears that Issac, the twin's father, is close to departing and longs to bless his firstborn, Esau. Isaac requests Esau hunt some of the wild gamey meats he craves and prepare them for him. Then Isaac will bless his firstborn. While Esau is out hunting, Mom gets meat prepared with herbs and bread, takes animal skins, and places them on Jacob, so he will appear hairy. Since Jacob's father's eyesight is dim, he can hardly see, so when he touches Jacob, he thinks it is Esau, and so, as the story goes, Jacob steals the birthright and the blessing. Isaac blesses Jacob, but Jacob is wearing Esau's clothing, disguised as him. Jacob does not know his true identity yet. How could a father not recognize the voice of his firstborn son?

> Behold, the smell of my son is like the smell of a field that Adonai has blessed. May God give you— from the dew of the sky and from the fatness of the land— an abundance of grain and new wine.
>
> May peoples serve you and may nations bow down to you. Be master over your brothers. May your mother's sons bow down to you. May those who curse you be cursed and may those who bless you be blessed.
>
> —Genesis 27: 28-29, TLV

Esau enters a bit later with his meat and wine and learns that not only has his brother cheated him out of his birthright, but now his blessing. Esau sold his birthright, but what does that mean? The Torah, the Book of Deuteronomy, demands a double portion of all the possessions be given to the firstborn son and forbids favor being shown to a younger son. Still, even the apostle Paul states that the older shall serve the younger. Why do we not read more about Isaac? Isaac is missing in most of the Torah. These are questions to ponder as we continue with Jacob's trouble and Esau's promise.

Esau wept, "bless me too father! Read carefully the proclamation given to Esau and his descendants:

> Isaac answered and said to Esau, "Behold, I've made him master over you, and all your brothers I've given to him as servants. I've provided him with grain and new wine. What then can I do for you, my son?"
>
> Esau said to his father, "Do you just have one blessing, my father? Bless me too, my father!" And Esau lifted up his voice and wept.
>
> Then Isaac his father said to him, "Behold, away from the land's fatness shall your dwelling be, away from the dew of the sky above. **By your sword shall you live, and your brother shall you serve. But when you tear yourself loose, you will tear his yoke off your neck."**
>
> —Genesis 27:37-40, BSB

As most Bible prophecies go, this has been fulfilled and can be fulfilled again. History repeats itself. There is nothing new under the sun. Abarim Publications, a Hebrew commentary, expounding on names and their meanings and breaks down Jacob and Esau as Edom and Israel and the yoke:

> Edom bordered Israel on the south and was a kingdom long before Israel (Genesis 36:31). Edom and Israel

skirmished throughout their existence. King Saul battled them (1 Samuel 14:47) but David conquered them (2 Samuel 8:14) and Edom remained under Israel's control until the reign of Jehoram (2 Kings 8:20).

The ethnonym אדמי, Edomite, occurs only sporadically in the Bible (Deuteronomy 23:8, 1 Samuel 21:8, 1 Kings 11:14), and is spelled without the signature letter *waw*. That means that Edomite is spelled the same as Adamite (one of Adam). In Greek times Edom became Idumea (spelled Ἰδουμαια and mentioned only in Mark 3:8) and the roles ironically reversed, since the Herod family was Idumean. [14]

We learn from the prophet Micah that the Holy One favored Jacob over Esau. After the death of his father, Isaac, Esau is ready to murder his deceitful brother. What can we learn or solve from Jacob's journey of trouble? Jacob's trouble continues until he breathes his last breath:

- Jacob leaves his mother and father. He is not there when his father dies, but he does receive his own blessing before exiting:
  "May God Almighty bless you and make you fruitful and multiply you, so that you may become

---

[14]https://www.abarim-publications.com/Meaning/Edom.html

a company of people. And may He give the blessing of Abraham to you and your descendants, so that you may possess the land where you dwell as a foreigner, the land God gave to Abraham" (Genesis 27:3-4, BSB). Afterward, Jacob travels to Paddan-Aram, and takes wives from the daughters of Laban.

- Jacob agrees to work seven years for Rachel, who he loves but receives her older sister on the wedding night. Jacob's eyes are as dim as his father's. Leah is veiled, and in the darkness, Jacob, like his father, Isaac, speaks lovingly over a woman who is not who he thinks she is. Laban is full of tricks, just like his sister, Jacob's mother, who convinced Jacob to go along with the scheme and not to worry, let the curses fall upon me; she says as she covers his hands in hairy garments. However, Rebbeca knew her oldest son did not care about the birthright, and she had been given the prophecy that the older would serve the younger years before. Jacob first marries Leah. Her name means cow or wild cow. Rachel means little Lamb. Jacob/Israel one day will marry the Lamb, Yeshua Messiah. Think prophecy and 7's. Kisha Gallagher, at *Grace in Torah* teaches the Biblical meanings of numbers in depth. Here is a portion from *Hebrew Numbers 1-10* concerning the number seven:

SEVEN: Shvah [f.], sheevah [m.] Rest, cessation from work, wholeness, completeness, being ripe, order, stability, and holiness. Also, the number of the Temple, Adonai's House. We rest (7) in the finished work (6) of the Messiah. There are seven days of creation, seven days for Temple dedication, seven Spirits of God, seven feasts of God, seven churches or assemblies in Revelation, seven stars in Yeshua's hand, seven golden lampstands, seven seals, seven trumpets, seven bowls, seven thunders that speak, seven eyes of the Lord, seven horns & eyes on the Lamb, seven abominations (wicked lamp spirits Pr. 6:16-19). [15]

Seven is the number of completion and rest:

- Continuing with Jacob's Trouble: After the wedding week with Leah is over, Jacob agrees to work 7 more years for Rachel. Now he is locked into a contract of 14 years of labor. Later, Jacob's son Joseph, the dream interpreter, will describe 7 fat cows and 7 skinny cows to warn of famine. Joseph's brothers will not recognize

---

[15] https://graceintorah.net/2015/06/15/hebrew-numbers-1-10/

him because he will be disguised as an Egyptian pharaoh. How many men are disguised in scripture? Too many! Even Jethro's daughters think Moses is an Egyptian. "An Egyptian rescued us from the shepherds," they replied. "He even drew water for us and watered the flock" (Exodus 2:19, BSB).

Continuing with Jacob's trouble:

- Esau said in his heart, "Let the time for mourning my father draw near, so that I can kill my brother Jacob!" (Genesis 27:41).

- Jacob/ Israel is so full of fear that his brother Esau/Edom will destroy him and murder his family, that he wrestles all night with an angel/Yeshua. His hip is now out of socket, and he humbly limps. Jacob devised a task to line up his family with his most precious cargo, Rachel and Joseph, in the rear. Jacob's trouble, stress, worry, fear, and anguish all come pouring forth to haunt him, but when Esau sees him, he is full of love and mercy. "Esau, however, ran to him and embraced him, threw his arms around his neck, and kissed him. And they both wept" (Genesis 33:4, BSB).

- Returning to Genesis 30, we learn that Jacob requests to leave Laban and his household. Through divination, Laban learns truth. Ponder and meditate on the verses. "But Laban replied, "If I have found favor in your eyes, please stay. I have learned by divination that the LORD has blessed me because of you" (Genesis 30:27, BSB). Jacob stays and acquires much livestock through epigenetics. With environmental influences, Jacob's striped and spotted livestock reproduce. Afterward, Jacob describes more of his troubles to his wives: "I can see from your father's countenance that his attitude toward me has changed; but the God of my father has been with me. You know that I have served your father with all my strength. **And although he has cheated me and changed my wages ten times, God has not allowed him to harm me**" (Genesis 31:5-7, BSB).

Traveling back to the reunion of Jacob and Esau, Jacob is petrified to face his brother Esau from whom he stole his birthright and blessings. This is when Jacob wrestles with a man all night, acquires a dislocated hip, and the new name, Israel. (Genesis 32). Remember, what Jacob sows, he reaps. Israel's first-born son is Reuben. His mother is Leah. Reuben sleeps with Bilhah, his father's concubine, the mother of his two half-brothers, Dan and Naphtali. (Genesis 35). More trouble and heartbreak.

- Jacob's second son is Simeon. Simeon and his brother Levi revenge the rape of their sister Dinah by Shechem. They are so filled with rage, they act with deception, call for all the males to be circumcised, then proceed by killing every male living in the city of Hamor (Genesis 34:25). Jacob now has much TROUBLE! "Three days later, while they were still in pain, two of Jacob's sons (Dinah's brothers Simeon and Levi) took their swords, went into the unsuspecting city, and slaughtered every male" (Genesis 34:25, BSB).

- Israel's third son is Levi. He also forfeits his status, along with his brother Simeon. "Jacob's other sons came upon the slaughter and looted the city, because their sister had been defiled. They took their flocks and herds and donkeys, and everything else in the city or in the field. They carried off all their possessions and women and children, and they plundered everything in their houses" (Genesis 34:27-29, BSB).

Follow along as we recount Jacob's life and his troubles. Imagine it on a worldwide scale. Men in power shaking hands, making a vow, then pillaging and murdering, taking women and children and wealth. These are the sons of Israel. And what does Jacob/Israel tell his household before they flee from Shechem? "Get rid of the foreign gods that are among you. Purify yourselves and change your garments" (Genesis 35:2, BSB):

- Israel's fourth son is Judah, and he is now ascending to a more prominent position in his family because of his brother's rage and destruction.

- After a season, Jacob and his family decide to leave Bethel. As they are traveling, Rachel, dark eyed beautiful lamb, the love of Israel's life, dies while giving birth. Rachel, in labor, calls him *Ben-oni*, "son of my sorrow," but Jacob/Israel names him, "Son of my right hand," Benjamin. Rachel dies and is buried on the way to Bethlehem.

- Later in the life of Jacob's troubles, his sons become very jealous of Joseph, the dreamer. The brothers decide to kill Joseph and throw him in a pit but are persuaded to sell him into slavery instead.

But no less, Joseph is headed to Egypt, and now Jacob will think his son, his firstborn son by Rachel, is dead. Jacob is told that wild animals have ravaged Joseph. Sadly, the wild animals were Jacob's own sons. The tunic Jacob made for Joseph is covered in blood. Israel, no doubt, remembers his father Isaac, whose father Abraham had taken his dad to a mountain, placed him bound on an altar, and raised a knife. The trauma of that event may have been the reason Jacob's father, Isaac, wanted nothing to do with Jacob. Isaac knew Jacob had the anointing and the longing for heavenly things, but Isaac also knew what that cost. By the time Israel ends up in Egypt, standing before Joseph, he speaks: "And Jacob saith unto Pharaoh, 'The days of the years of my sojourning's are an hundred and thirty years; few and evil have been the days of the years of my life, and they have not reached the days of the years of the life of my fathers, in the days of their sojourning's" (Genesis 47:9, YLT).

Now, I have told you all these things to say this. The whole story is a layered journey concerning the Patriarchs and the Matriarchs. It involves outside disputes, murder, stealing, robbing, pillaging, idols, bad blood with family, and more bad events with wives' families. Hatred, jealousy, and adultery were in the hearts of Jacob's own seed. It is trouble after trouble. If I were a guessing gal, I would even state that most women have felt like Leah and Rachel. If we were to describe nations using Jacob's seed as world leaders, we would be close to seeing a greater picture. Many theologians will tell you the *Days of Awe or Jacob's Trouble* have already come forth. Trouble happens in all generations. There is so much trouble going on with the men and women in the Old Testament/Torah; they all need therapy, deliverance, healing, rebuke, and a fear of Adonai. We are told again and again that those who overcome will be saved. Saved from what? Jacob's trouble:

> He who overcomes will thus be clothed in white garments; and I will not erase his name from the book of life, and I

will confess his name before My Father and before His angels.

—Revelation 3:5, NASB

Can our names be blotted out of His Book?

Let them be blotted out of the book of the living, and not be written with the righteous.

—Psalms 69:28, KJB

And the LORD said unto Moses, Whosoever hath sinned against me, him will I blot out of my book.

—Exodus 32:32, KJB

Nevertheless, do not rejoice because the spirits are subject to you, but rejoice because your names are written in heaven.

—Luke 10:20, NASB

Yes, and I ask you, my true yokefellow, to help these women who have labored with me for the gospel, along with Clement and the rest of my fellow workers, whose names are in the Book of Life.

—Philippians 4:3, BSB

At that time Michael, the great prince who stands watch over your people, will rise up. There will be a time of distress, the likes of which will not have occurred from the beginning of nations until that time. But at that time your people—everyone whose name is found written in the book—will be delivered.

—Daniel 12:1, BSB

When discussing Jacob's Trouble, most point to Daniel 9. This is one of the most taught passages concerning end time prophecy. Daniel was studying and reading the scrolls of Jeremiah and Isaiah. The prophet Daniel was trying to calculate if the 70 years had been fulfilled for his people concerning the exile. While engrossed in study and prayer, an angelic messenger brings a prophecy to Daniel:

> While I, Daniel, was watching the vision and trying to understand it, there stood before me one having the appearance of a man. And I heard the voice of a man calling from between the banks of the Ulai: "Gabriel, explain the vision to this man."
>
> As he came near to where I stood, I was terrified and fell facedown. "Son of man," he said to me, "understand that the vision concerns the time of the end."

—Daniel 8:15-17, BSB

Many scholars believe Daniel 8 refers to Antiochus IV Epiphanes, an Antichrist. The Book of Daniel expounds on the seven years of tribulation and the 3 ½ mark. Daniel 9 gives a timeline:

Seventy weeks are decreed for your people and your holy city to stop their transgression, to put an end to sin, to make atonement for iniquity, to bring in everlasting righteousness, to seal up vision and prophecy, and to anoint the Most Holy Place.

Know and understand this: From the issuance of the decree to restore and rebuild Jerusalem, until the Messiah, the Prince, there will be seven weeks and sixty-two weeks. It will be rebuilt with streets and a trench, but in times of distress. Then after the sixty-two weeks the Messiah will be cut off and will have nothing.

Then the people of the prince who is to come will destroy the city and the sanctuary. The end will come like a flood, and until the end there will be war; desolations have been decreed. And he will confirm a covenant with many for one week, but in the middle of the week he will put an end to sacrifice and offering. And on the wing of the temple will come the abomination that causes desolation, until the decreed destruction is poured out upon him."

—Daniel 9:24-27, TLV

The term "Messiah" is also translated as the Anointed One in other Bible translations. Why is this important? The reason being is the words 'anointed one' can refer to High Priest, kings, and prophets, but no need to squabble, Daniel 7 explains the One who is anointed, Messiah, Yeshua:

In my vision in the night I continued to watch, and I saw One like the Son of Man coming with the clouds of heaven. He approached the Ancient of Days and was led into His presence. And He was given dominion, glory, and kingship, that the people of every nation and language should serve Him. His dominion is an everlasting dominion that will not pass away, and His kingdom is one that will never be destroyed.

—Daniel 7:13-14, BSB

A careful reading of the Book of Daniel gives future events that are horrific. In 167, three years after the murder of Onias, the ultimate desecration ensued in Jerusalem. Antiochus rose up with his army and against the temple. He abolished the daily sacrifice and set up the abomination that causes desolation. Antiochus plundered the temple and dedicated the sanctuary to Zeus by sacrificing a swine on the altar.

To understand the "weeks" mentioned in the Book of Daniel, we need only look at the famine during King Ahab: Elijah was a man just like us. He prayed earnestly that it would not rain, and it did not rain on the land for three and a half years. (James 5:17). This is the 3 ½ mark. This is the middle of the week. A week being 7 years. "The beast was given a mouth to speak arrogant and blasphemous words, and authority to act for 42 months. (3 ½ years)" (Revelation 13:5, BSB).

Paul Tanner, author and scholar, defends the prophecies from Daniel against the naysayers who suggest Daniel 9:25 is not concerning the Messiah but instead must be referring to Cyrus, the High Priest, Zerubbabel, or Joshua son of Jehozadak, all from the sixth century B.C. Tanner expounds on the Hebrew text, and the entire document is worthy of further investigation. See footnote for the two-part exegesis:

> Daniel's prayerful confession and plea on behalf of the nation in Daniel 9 began with his reading Jeremiah 25:11–12 and 29:10 that the nation's exile in and servitude to Babylon would end after seventy years (not after 490 years) and the Babylonian king would be punished. Judah lost her independence in 609 B.C. when Pharaoh Neco II of Egypt killed King Josiah and Judah became a vassal state of Egypt, only to be made a vassal state of Babylon four years later. In 539 B.C.—seventy years later—Babylon was overthrown, and the prophecy of Jeremiah was literally fulfilled. Daniel hoped that Jerusalem's desolations would be complete with Babylon's downfall, but the Lord showed him that seventy sevens of years would still be needed for her desolations to be fulfilled. Since the latter was established on a foundation of seventy literal years, logically the extended period should be viewed as literal as well.

Daniel's prayer in 9:4–19 was based on his expectation of exile for a literal seventy years. The divine response to his prayer was that an extended period of God's chastening on the nation would transpire not in seventy years, but in seventy times seven years. If the first period of the Exile was literal, one should expect the extended chastisement to be literal also. Even early Jewish views of Daniel, both before and after A.D. 70, followed a literal understanding of the years involved. Daniel 9:24–27 is a glorious messianic revelation of the Lord Jesus Christ, announcing among other things the time of His coming and His death before the cataclysmic events of A.D. 70. The passage remains a bedrock of prophetic revelation. [16]

There are four main interpretations of these passages from the Book of Daniel. I will not go into extensive details. My book is predominantly about the festivals/moedim listed in Leviticus 23, and I am not an Eschatology expert.

In our next chapter, we will explore the Day of Atonement/ Yom Kippur and a prayer said while standing, the Amidah.

16

https://paultanner.org/English%20HTML/Publ%20Articles/Daniel%27s%207
0th%20Wk%20-%20BibSac%20Article%202%20-%20Dr%20Tanner.pdf

The Day of Atonement or

Yom HaKippurim

Part 3

The Day of Atonement, named *Yom Kippur* in Hebrew, is the sixth feast in our series. The word *Kippur* is Strong's #3725, meaning to make atonement, wipe out, and to cover. The Day of Atonement is a day set aside to afflict one's soul—a time of introspection. During the nine days leading up to the 10th day, the Day of Atonement, the Jewish people spend time making things right with anyone they may have wronged or hurt. The Sages believe the actual day, the tenth day of Yom Kippur, is the day that Adam sinned and was removed from the Garden of Eden, and it is also thought to be the day when Israel will be restored. These beliefs refer to *midrash*, a Jewish mode of interpretation:

> ADONAI said to Moshe, "The tenth day of this seventh month is Yom-Kippur; you are to have a holy convocation, you are to deny yourselves, and you are to bring an offering made by fire to ADONAI. You are not to do any

kind of work on that day, because it is Yom-Kippur, to make atonement for you before ADONAI your God. Anyone who does not deny himself on that day is to be cut off from his people; and anyone who does any kind of work on that day, I will destroy from among his people."

—Leviticus 23:27-30, CJB

Again, the people can do no work. This day of rest reflects our righteousness, which is not acquired by works but by faith through grace and the blood of Yeshua.

The last prayer on the Day of Atonement, a prayer said standing, holds a significant connection to a parable given by the Messiah in Luke 18. This parable, it is implied, is a reflection on the Day of Atonement:

Two men went up into the temple to pray, one a Pharisee and the other a tax collector. "The Pharisee stood and was praying this to himself: 'God, I thank You that I am not like other people: swindlers, unjust, adulterers, or even like this tax collector. I fast twice a week; I pay tithes of all that I get.' "But the tax collector, standing some distance away, was even unwilling to lift up his eyes to heaven, but was beating his breast, saying, 'God, be merciful to me, the sinner!'"

—Luke 18:10-13, NASB

If we know the history of our faith or the traditions, we can understand important messages hidden in scripture. The beating of the breast happened during the Day of Atonement and during a prayer that was said called the *Viddui* (confession):

> During the Viddui, worshipers gently beat themselves on the chest for each transgression listed. This action serves as a symbolic punishment for our hearts, which are ultimately responsible for leading us to sins of greed, lust and anger. [17]

The prayer Viddui is spoken in humility by the Jewish people, with the plea to come before the King of Glory. It is an admittance that they are not so arrogant and stiff-necked as to think that they are completely righteous and have not erred. In Luke 18, Yeshua is referring to this standing prayer and the light tapping or beating on the breast while speaking it.

In Luke 23, the people in one accord shout, "Crucify Him!," concerning Yeshua. Pilate and Herod continue to explain that they find no fault or reason why Yeshua should be crucified, but the people again respond and prevail: "But they were insistent, demanding with loud voices for Jesus to be crucified. And their clamor prevailed" (Luke 23:23, BSB). After He is crucified, we read of the earth quaking and the veil in the Temple is torn in half. According to Josephus one of the veils was 4 inches thick. It

---

[17] The Yom Kippur Confession (Viddui) | My Jewish Learning

is after this that the people begin to do what they do during the Viddui prayer, they beat their breasts: "And when all the people who had gathered for this spectacle saw what had happened, they returned home beating their breasts" (Luke 23:48, BSB).

The most intriguing words spoken during these prayers on Yom Kippur are words requesting that the gates will not be shut and that they may enter into the presence of the Almighty. Yeshua mentions this gate/door in Luke 13:

> "Strive to enter through the narrow gate, because many, I say to you, shall seek to enter in and shall not be able. When once the Master of the house has risen up and shut the door, and you begin to stand outside and knock at the door, saying, 'Master, Master, open for us,' and He shall answer and say to you, "I do not know you, where you are from," when you shall begin to say, 'We ate and drank in Your presence, and You taught in our streets.' "But He shall say, 'I say to you I do not know you, where you are from. Depart from Me, all you workers of unrighteousness."
>
> —Luke 13:24-27, ISR

Those mentioned in Luke 13 act as if they know the Messiah and do much ministry, but He claims they were workers of lawlessness and that there would be much weeping and gnashing of teeth outside those gates. We must be careful that Yeshua does not find us naked trying to enter through a wide gate the whole world is privy to and not the narrow gate.

In Revelation 8, the 7th seal is broken, and an eerie silence is said to take place upon the earth:

> When the Lamb broke the seventh seal there was silence in heaven for what seemed like half an hour. Then I saw the seven angels who stand before God, and they were given seven shofars.
>
> —Revelation 8:1-2, CJB

Reading the whole chapter of Revelation 8 reveals that each shofar brings great woes, and by the time the reader gets to Chapter 10, something curious happens, seven thunders speak:

> Then I saw another mighty angel coming down from heaven. He was robed in a cloud, with a rainbow above his head; his face was like the sun, and his legs were like fiery pillars. He was holding a little scroll, which lay open in his hand. He planted his right foot on the sea and his left foot on the land, and he gave a loud shout like the roar of a lion. When he shouted, the voices of the seven thunders spoke. And when the seven thunders spoke, I was about to write; but I heard a voice from heaven say, "Seal up what the seven thunders have said and do not write it down."
>
> —Revelation 10:1-4, CJB

Thunder in the natural is followed by lightning, and this combination represents the voice of Adonai. This scene is reminiscent of the giving of the Torah in Exodus 19:

> In the morning of the third day, there was thundering and lightning, a thick cloud on the mountain, and the blast of an exceedingly loud *shofar*. All the people in the camp trembled. Then Moses brought the people out of the camp to meet God, and they stood at the lowest part of the mountain. Now the entire Mount Sinai was in smoke, because *Adonai* had descended upon it in fire. The smoke ascended like the smoke of a furnace. The whole mountain quaked greatly. When the sound of the *shofar* grew louder and louder, Moses spoke, and God answered him with a thunderous sound.
>
> —Exodus 19:16-19, CJB

Adonai's Voice thunders and causes men to quake. Job, Jeremiah, David, and others confirm this:

> Behold, these are the fringes of His ways; and how faint a word we hear of Him! But His mighty thunder, who can understand?
>
> —Job 26:14, NASB

> And can you thunder with a voice like His?
>
> —Job 40:9, NASB

The voice of the LORD is upon the waters; The God of glory thunders, The LORD is over many waters.

—Psalm 29:3, NASB

In Revelation 10, the voice of the seven (7) thunders spoke, but John was told to seal up the words. Backing up, in Revelation 8, we read of more lightning and thunder. The prayers of the Saints were likened to an offering made by fire:

> Then another angel, who had a golden censer, came and stood at the altar. He was given much incense to offer, along with the prayers of all the saints, on the golden altar before the throne. And the smoke of the incense, together with the prayers of the saints, rose up before God from the hand of the angel.
>
> Then the angel took the censer, filled it with fire from the altar, and hurled it to the earth; and there were peals of thunder, and rumblings, and flashes of lightning, and an earthquake.
>
> —Revelation 8:3-5, BSB

After the angels hurl this fire to the earth, suddenly the waters, liken to the plagues in Egypt, turn to blood. Not only that, but locusts appear. What could the thirty minutes of silence be? This thirty minute of silence may represent part of a ritual performed during the Day of Atonement when the High Priest went behind the veil to offer penance for the sins of the people. The Holy One sealed this, so no one knows what the exact meaning is. "Seal up what the seven thunders have said and do not write it down" (Revelation 10:4, BSB).

"When the Lamb broke the seventh seal there was silence in heaven for what seemed like half an hour" (Revelation 8:1, CJB). Today in Israel during this holiest day of the year, Yom Kippur, there is silence across the land as people humble themselves and pray:

> The two incense priests mount the twelve steps that lead to the Sanctuary building and they enter the Holy Place. At a signal from the Overseer, the priest gently places the incense on the altar, "like sifting grains of flour" and as the Holy Place fills with smoke he prostrates himself then leaves the Sanctuary.
>
> All those outside are waiting in a reverent hush, just as they did when the father of John the Baptist delayed his exit from the Sanctuary. (Luke 1:21)
>
> It is a recorded fact of the Temple service that the whole process of collecting the fire from the altar, offering the incense, and re-emerging from the Sanctuary took thirty minutes. [18]

---

[18] https://bannerministries.wordpress.com/2015/04/20/why-half-an-hours-silence-in-heaven/

What happens to John the Immerser's father after offering the incense? Zechariah becomes mute, silent. He cannot speak, and his lips are not loosened until John is born. The incense always comes first and precedes everything. For this reason, the section of the incense comes before prayer, hymns, and praises. For nothing rises, is perfected or connected, before filth is removed.

During this time, the musical and vocal praises in the Temple ceased, and the people stood in an awed silence without a word spoken for half an hour. The astounding revelation connected with this concerns a day called the 8th Day, which is celebrated after Sukkot. It represents a time of our reign with the Messiah—a season of joy that is unspeakable. We will cover that in a closing chapter. Notice Zechariah's silence turns to joy on the 8th day:

> On the eighth day, when they came to circumcise the child, they were going to name him after his father Zechariah. But his mother replied, "No! He shall be called John."
>
> They said to her, "There is no one among your relatives who bears this name." So they made signs to his father to find out what he wanted to name the child.
>
> Zechariah asked for a tablet and wrote, "His name is John." And they were all amazed. Immediately Zechariah's mouth was opened and his tongue was released, and he began to speak, praising God.
>
> —Luke 1:59-64, BSB

> He who overcomes will thus be clothed in white garments; and I will not erase his name from the book of life, and I will confess his name before My Father and before His angels.
>
> —Revelation 3:5, NASB

What happens to those whose names are not recorded in the Lamb's Book of Life?

> And if anyone's name was not found written in the book of life, he was thrown into the lake of fire.
>
> —Revelation 20:15, NASB

The last portion of the Book of Revelation renders who is allowed into the New Kingdom:

> And nothing unclean, and no one who practices abomination and lying, shall ever come into it, but only those whose names are written in the Lamb's book of life.
>
> —Revelation 21:27, NASB

The Day of Atonement or Yom HaKippurim

Part 4

The Scapegoat Offering

As with all the feast days, the scapegoat offering, and the Day of Atonement have hidden meanings and Revelation concerning Yeshua. We first read about the scapegoats in Leviticus:

> He shall take the two goats and present them before the LORD at the doorway of the tent of meeting. "Aaron shall cast lots for the two goats, one lot for the LORD and the other lot for the scapegoat. "Then Aaron shall offer the goat on which the lot for the LORD fell, and make it a sin offering. "But the goat on which the lot for the scapegoat fell shall be presented alive before the LORD, to make atonement upon it, to send it into the wilderness as the scapegoat.
>
> —Leviticus 16:7-10, NASB

The scapegoat was sacrificed on the Day of Atonement. This feast called "Yom Kippur" means simply "The Day." This is the day Adonai covered their sins. The High Priest would bathe, dress in pure white garments, walk barefoot to the temple and offer a young bullock as a sin offering for himself and his household. He had to cleanse himself before he could offer sacrifices for the people. On this day he was a humble priest, removing his gold head plate or frontlet. He would take off his colorful jeweled priestly garments that were detailed and adorned with gemstones. These were all exchanged for pure white linen. Our Yeshua was stripped of his clothes and given a crown of thorns as he hung naked. His Kingly garments were set aside.

After the priest offered his own sacrifice for his sins, he selected two young goats. These animals had to be exact. The goats were to look like identical twins. The two goats were presented to Adonai, and inside an urn, there were two lots. One lot for each goat and depending on how the lots fell, one goat was called the Lord's goat, and one was called the scapegoat. The lots were marked "For HaShem (the Name)" and "For Azazel." Many teach that Azazel is Satan, but is he?

> According to the Jewish encyclopedia, "Azazel¬¬ in Rabbinic Judaism, it is not a name of an entity but rather means literally 'for the complete removal,' i.e.,

designating the goat to be cast out into the wilderness as opposed to the goat sacrificed 'for YHWH.'" [19]

Strong's Hebrew Concordance #5799 is the Hebrew word *Azazel*, and it means the entire removal. [20]

Two goats were presented on Yom Kippur, and there were two men led before Pilate to determine their fate. One man would be set free, the other crucified. Ironically, both of the men had almost the same name:

> Now at the feast, the governor was accustomed to release for the people any one prisoner whom they wanted. At that time they were holding a notorious prisoner, called Barabbas. So when the people gathered together, Pilate said to them, "Whom do you want me to release for you? Barabbas, or Jesus who is called Christ?" For he knew that because of envy they had handed Him over.
>
> —Matthew 27:15-18, NASB

---

[19] http://www.jewishencyclopedia.com/articles/2203-azazel

[20] https://biblehub.com/str/hebrew/5799.htm

"Barabbas or Jesus Barabbas (a Hellenization of the Aramaic bar abba בר אבא, literally "son of the father" or "Jesus, son of the Father" respectively).' [21]

In Matthew 27:16 they referred to Barabbas as a well-known prisoner. In Mark 15 a murderer: "And there was one called Barabba, chained with his fellow rebels, who had committed murder in the uprising" (Mark 15:7, ISR). In Luke 23, we learn that Barabbas had committed murder during the insurrection against the occupying Roman forces. John 18:40 describes him as a robber or thief.

Hebrew Streams, a scholarly website, explains more concerning the name Barabbas:

> Many textual scholars believe the double name "Jesus Barabbas" was the original reading. They suggest that "Jesus" was omitted from several Greek manuscripts of Matthew out of reverence. [22]

During the Day of Atonement, there were two goats, and before the crucifixion, there were two men who stood before Pilate. One man was a man full of sin, Barabbas, and the other

---

[21] Barabbas | The amazing name Barabbas: meaning and etymology (abarim-publications.com)

[22] Hebrew Streams: Yeshua bar Abba & Barabbas (hebrew-streams.org)

was our Messiah. Pilate assumed the people would let Yeshua go, but he was wrong. The one who was a criminal was set free. Yeshua took our sins that day on the cross and freed us from death by being a sacrifice for us. Many believe this is a picture of the two goats. One goat took all the sins of the people, and one was set free in the wilderness or pushed off a cliff. Again, many denominations and teachers take this further and say that Azazel is Satan or the devil. (For more on Satan see Book One of my four-part series, *Satan Unmasked*.)

I disagree with those who consider Azazel as Satan. Remember both goats had to be similar in height, appearance, and value. Both goats took the sins of the people. The embodiment of Satan as taught by theologians would never take the sins of the people. Yeshua was led by the Spirit into the wilderness to be tempted by the adversary. Yeshua was able to overcome each temptation by using the Word (*Torah*) to obtain the victory. He also took all our sins:

> And He was in the wilderness forty days being tempted by Satan; and He was with the wild beasts, and the angels were ministering to Him.
>
> —Mark 1:13, NASB

One goat was taken to the wilderness, and he took all the sins of the people just as Yeshua did. If Yeshua had not been able to defeat the adversary in the wilderness, he would not have been acceptable to be sacrificed for our sins. Could it be possible that both of these goats represent our Messiah? One goat was for the people, and one goat was for *HaShem* (His Father):

> In order to ensure that the two goats—which were identical in appearance—would not become confused with one another, the *Kohen Gadol* [High Priest] would tie a red woolen strip to the head of the goat for Azazel, and another strip around the neck of the sin-offering. When the goat for Azazel was pushed over the precipice, the red wool would miraculously turn white, to symbolize that Israel's sins had been forgiven (Yoma 39a). [23]

One goat had all the sins of the nation placed upon it, and after the words of the High Priest went forth, it was said to be spiritually dead. In my opinion, this is also a picture of a loving Father, leaving our sin and bondage in the wilderness of Egypt and pushing the goat off the cliff, ensuring it would never find its way back into the camp. We, too, must leave our bondage and sin in Egypt and die a spiritual death.

Yeshua said:

---

[23] Yoma 39a (sefaria.org)

Truly, truly, I say to you, unless a grain of wheat falls into the earth and dies, it remains alone; but if it dies, it bears much fruit.

—John 12:24, NASB

Come now, let us settle the matter," says the LORD. "Though your sins are like scarlet, they shall be as white as snow; though they are red as crimson, they shall be like wool.

—Isaiah 1:18, NIV

According to the *Talmud* [compilation of ancient teachings regarded as sacred in Judaism], a strip of red wool was placed on the temple door, as well as on the Azazel goat. Each year the cloth would turn snow white as a sign that Adonai had forgiven His people. This annual event happened until 30 A.D.

Jerusalem Talmud:

"Forty years before the destruction of the Temple, the western light went out, the crimson thread remained crimson, and the lot for the Lord always came up in the left hand. They would close the gates of the Temple by night and get up in the morning and find them wide open" (Jacob Neusner, The Yerushalmi, p.156-157). [the Temple was destroyed in 70 CE]

Babylonian Talmud:

> Our rabbis taught: During the last forty years before the destruction of the Temple the lot [For the Lord] did not come up in the right hand; nor did the crimson-colored strap become white; nor did the western most light shine; and the doors of the *Hekel* [Temple] would open by themselves (Soncino version, Yoma 39b).

Window View website offers statistics and insight on what happened after the death and resurrection of the Messiah, *Talmudic Evidence for the Messiah at 30 C.E*:

> During the two hundred years before 30 CE, when the High Priest picked one of two stones (lots), again this selection was governed by chance, and each year the priest would select a black stone as often as a white stone. But for forty years in a row, beginning in 30 CE, the High Priest always picked the black stone. The odds against this happening are astronomical (2 to the 40th power). In other words, the chances of this occurring are 1 in approximately 1,099,511,627,776 — or over one trillion to one. [24]

---

[24] Talmudic Evidence for Messiah at 30 CE - Unique Events Identify Messiah (windowview.org)

Yeshua died and arose from the grave. Death could not hold Him. The Temple doors could not Hold Him. He was and is the Light of the world:

> But Christ has indeed been raised from the dead, the firstfruits of those who have fallen asleep. For since death came through a man, the resurrection of the dead comes also through a man. For as in Adam all die, so in Christ all will be made alive. But each in his own turn: Christ the firstfruits; then at His coming, those who belong to Him.
>
> Then the end will come, when He hands over the kingdom to God the Father after He has destroyed all dominion, authority, and power. For He must reign until He has put all His enemies under His feet. The last enemy to be destroyed is death.
>
> —I Corinthians 15:20-26, BSB

The Day of Atonement or

Yom HaKippurim

Part 5

Yom Kippur and the days leading up to the feast are a time of introspection; I want to expound on what lies in our bellies. This chapter is a bit of a paradox concerning life, death, and the most sacred place of all: the womb. In II Kings 15, we have a king who rips the unborn from the womb. Ironically, this King's name means "consoling—comforter."

> At that time Menahem, starting from Tirzah, attacked Tiphsah and everyone in its vicinity, because they would not open their gates. So he attacked Tiphsah and ripped open all the pregnant women.
>
> —II Kings 15:16, BSB

Menahem did these things because the gates and doors would not open to him. Tiphsah would not let him in to usurp the kingdom, so he took it by force. Tirzah was one of the seven daughters of Zelophehad, the son of Hepher of the tribe of

Manasseh. Tirzah brought a change in Mosaic hereditary laws. God granted her an inheritance with the men. Both places Menahem invaded and destroyed had meaning: Strong's Hebrew 8607: Tiphsah– (crossing over):

1. Menahem came to bring chaos and remove comfort.

2. Menahem came to destroy life.

3. Menahem came to usurp a king.

4. Menahem came to murder.

5. Menahem came to stop people from crossing over (bridge).

The cruel acts of Menahem were to cut life from the womb!

The days of Elul are known as days of Teshuva (repentance), from the word *LaShuv* to return to ourselves, our soul, our identity, and our inner connection. Yes, that is Elul, but the prior month is the month of Av. On the 9th of the Hebrew month of Av, Titus and his army forces broke through the city walls and commenced a great slaughter of those left inside the Temple. According to Josephus, a river of blood flowed down the Temple stairs. Before they set fire to the Temple, the legionaries made pagan sacrifices on the holy altars. Josephus describes the destruction of the Temple:

> While the holy house (The Temple) was on fire, everything was plundered that came to hand, and ten thousand of

those that were caught were slain; nor was there a commiseration of any age, but children and old men and priests, were all slain in the same manner. The flame was also carried a long way and made an echo, together with the groans of those who were slain. . . one would have thought the whole city would have been on fire. Nor can one imagine anything greater and more terrible than this noise. [25]

The Temple, the place of life, was filled with death. The sound of death echoing in the place of life is very grievous. Just as Menahem cut out the life of the womb, The Holy One allowed the destruction of the first and second temple over idolatry and baseless hatred. During this season, we ask the Father if we have baseless hatred for anyone. Do we have echoes of bitterness and unforgiveness? Does death echo loudly inside our houses— our temples?

Speaking of birth, Yeshua said we must be born again or rather born from above. A heavenly birth. A spiritual awakening. Evil Menahem's name means comfort. What if the Holy Spirit, the true Comforter, came to help us cut some of the past year's fleshly nature out of our bellies?

---

[25] https://ccel.org/ccel/josephus/complete.iii.vii.v.html

The acts of the flesh are obvious: sexual immorality, impurity, and debauchery; idolatry and sorcery; hatred, discord, jealousy, and rage; rivalries, divisions, factions, and envy; drunkenness, orgies, and the like. I warn you, as I did before, that those who practice such things will not inherit the kingdom of God.

—Galatians 5:19-21, BSB

We often look at some of the fruits we deem more serious and think, well, I don't do that. But fits of anger make the list. What pictures come to mind when you envision someone throwing a fit? For me, it's a toddler stomping and kicking, throwing toys, and crying over not getting their way:

1. A wrathful man stirs up discord, but one slow to anger calms strife (Proverbs 15:18).
2. He who is slow to anger is better than the mighty, and he who rules his spirit is better than he who takes a city (Proverbs 16:32).

Menahem could take over a city and a kingdom, but he could not rule his own spirit.

In Galatians 5, division made the list. Division is something we see today in families, in assemblies, and in America. A house divided cannot stand. A nation divided cannot stand. Strife is discord and bitter arguments that lead to division and often with no closure or healing. What if hatred, discord, jealousy, and rage;

rivalries, divisions, factions, and envy were cut out of our wombs by the Comforter—by the fire of the Holy Spirit burning our tongues with purifying fire and cleansing our eyes with eye salve?

What if new life could be birthed? What if the sword of the Spirit was held by the Comforter who gently cut and circumcised our flesh away. Can you picture our ugly flesh in our bellies being cut out? If me and my siblings were fighting, my mother used to say, "Cut it out, you two!" What if our wombs had death cut out by His sword—the Word of Yahweh:

> For the word of God is living and active. Sharper than any double-edged sword, it pierces even to dividing soul and spirit, joints and marrow. It judges the thoughts and intentions of the heart. Nothing in all creation is hidden from God's sight; everything is uncovered and exposed before the eyes of Him to whom we must give account.
>
> —Hebrews 4:12-13, BSB

The Holy One knows what we are birthing. What if we began to birth life—beautiful life? No ugly babies! No bad fruit. The fruit of the Spirit is worth meditating on. Each piece of juicy fruit is LIFE sustaining:

> But the fruit of the Spirit is love, joy, peace, patience, kindness, goodness, faithfulness, gentleness, self-control; against such things, there is no law. And those who belong to Christ Jesus have crucified the flesh with its passions

and desires. If we live by the Spirit, let us also keep in step with the Spirit. Let us not become conceited, provoking one another, envying one another.

—Galatians 5:22-26, BSB

Author and teacher Brad Scott explains more about life:

There are two Hebrew words that are translated as the word womb in Scripture. One is beten (בטן) and is used commonly to express the area of the belly. The other word is used exclusively to speak of the home of the first nine months of a child. This word is rechem (רחם). Rechem is from the root racham, and is, in its root, the word for compassion and mercy. Its root meaning is "**protection from harm**." [26]

Oh, the Holy One wants to PROTECT US FROM HARM. He wants to gather us under His Wings, His Truths, and cause us to eat from the Tree of Life.

We must protect what He is birthing in our wombs by placing boundaries so that we are not invaded. Of course, we know that no man can tame the tongue, but we can sure use our tongues to spread life, honey, His Word, and mercy to those who need it, and when we see someone giving birth to what would

---

[26] https://www.wildbranch.org/

seem an ugly baby, we can cause them to "cut it out," like our Mother (Holy Spirit) would say to us:

> But the wisdom from above is first of all pure, then peace-loving, gentle, accommodating, full of mercy and good fruit, impartial, and sincere. Peacemakers who sow in peace reap the fruit of righteousness.
>
> —James 3:17, BSB

Fruit is a part of the Feast of Yom Kippur. Looking inward and trying to do inventory like a good accountant. Around 15 years ago, I entered a Yom Kippur service at a synagogue where everyone in the room was mainly wearing white. I came dressed in black and received quite a few second looks. I had no knowledge of Jewish customs or traditions that I should be dressed in the white robes of the Saints mentioned in Revelation 3:

> But you do have a few people in Sardis who have not soiled their garments, and because they are worthy, they will walk with Me in white. Like them, he who overcomes will be dressed in white. And I will never blot out his name from the Book of Life, but I will confess his name before My Father and His angels.
>
> —Revelation 3:4-5, BSB

Tradition states that Moses made his way up to Mt. Sinai (Ex. 24:18) on the Day of Pentecost when he was given the tablets or

Ten Commandments. When Moses went up on the mountain, the Glory cloud settled on the mountain for six days, and on the seventh day the Holy One called to Moses from within the cloud. Moses under the power and Breath of the Lord (YHVH) stayed on the mountain in the cloud for 40 days and 40 nights. It is after this that the Holy One speaks to Moses concerning the golden calf, and Moses pleads for the people and returns for yet 40 more days and nights without bread or water. (See Dt. 9:18-25). Moses actually returns for a total of 8 times which includes the burning bush in Exodus 3.

After the Exodus account, we learn more about the Day of Atonement, also referred to as the "Day of at one ment." Many of the Jewish people feel an exceptional sense of release and spiritual unity after repentance and forgiveness. The Day of Atonement, known as Yom Kippur, was the only day that the High Priest could enter the Holy of Holies. The High Priest had to make Atonement for the people's sins. First, he had to make Atonement for himself. Leviticus 16 goes into all the bloody details:

> He [Aaron] is then to take some of the blood of the bull and sprinkle it with his finger on the atonement cover, on the east side. Before the atonement cover he is to sprinkle some of the blood with his finger seven times. Then he is to slaughter the goat of the sin offering which is for the people, bring its blood behind the curtain, and do with it

as he did with the blood of the bull—sprinkle it upon the atonement cover, and before the atonement cover. So he is to make atonement for the Holy Place, because of the uncleanness of *Bnei-Yisrael* and because of their transgressions, all their sins. He is to do the same for the Tent of Meeting, which dwells with them in the midst of their impurities.

—Leviticus 16:14-16, TLV

In all the other feasts, the people were given instructions such as removing yeast from their dwelling places, and eating the Passover lamb. In the Feast of Trumpets, they were to blow shofars and during the Feast of Sukkot or Tabernacles they were instructed on how to build a sukkah and camp outside for a week. Yes, directions are given in all the other feasts pertaining to Yeshua but not on Yom Kippur. In Leviticus 16, all the people could do was humble themselves and do no work. The people were told to afflict their souls, meaning "fast." Aaron the High Priest had to bathe, change garments, and offer the incense, the burnt offering, and the sprinkling of the blood. Meanwhile, the people waited, and they are still waiting. Each year during this season, many pray for brother Judah to see the Messiah. Praise be to our Messiah Yeshua, who went once and for all behind the veil:

And every priest stands ministering daily and offering repeatedly the same sacrifices, which can never take away sins. But this Man, after He had offered one sacrifice for sins forever, sat down at the right hand of God, from that time waiting till His enemies are made His footstool. For by one offering He has perfected forever those who are being sanctified.

—Hebrews 10:11-14, NKJV

For by grace you have been saved through faith. And this is not from yourselves—it is the gift of God. It is not based on deeds, so that no one may boast. For we are His workmanship—created in Messiah *Yeshua* for good deeds, which God prepared beforehand so we might walk in them.

—Ephesians 2:8-10, TLV

First Aaron offered the incense and created the fragrant cloud. Next, Aaron was to sprinkle the blood of the purification— first the bull, then the goat. The Book of Hebrew, tells us Yeshua went once and offered up his life. He was unlike Aaron, a High Priest who had to go behind the veil and offer sacrifices for himself and the people, not knowing if he would live or die year after year:

For such a *Kohen Gadol* (High Priest) was fitting for us: holy, guiltless, undefiled, separated from sinners, and exalted above the heavens. He has no need to offer up sacrifices day by day like those other kohanim g'dolim—

first for their own sins and then for the sins of the people. For when He offered up Himself, He did this once for all.

—Hebrews 7:26-27, TLV

Hallelujah! Praise be to His wonderful Name!

On Yom Kippur, many Jews and Christians stand and lightly beat or tap upon their breast while repeating prayers—prayers that cover every sin imaginable. Some fast, no food or drink for 24 hours. Afterwards, at sundown, a joyous meal is shared. If you want to fast during this festival, please consult your doctor.

In the Book of Isaiah, God's people were keeping Yom Kippur with dull, dead hearts, and treating their hired laborers with cruelty. They were neglecting the poor, the widows, and those in their own families. They were proudly walking in their religious arrogance. They ask the Holy One why He does not see them. Why doesn't He notice their fast? The prophet Isaiah is given a harsh message to deliver to God's people. The bullet points below break down the main issues:

- You seek your own pleasure.
- You exploit all your laborers.
- You fast for strife and contention.
- You make your own voice heard.

"Why have we fasted. yet You do not see? Why have we afflicted our souls, yet You take no notice?"

"Behold, in the day of your fast you seek your own pleasure, and exploit all your laborers. Behold, you fast for strife and contention and to strike with a wicked fist. You should not fast as you do today to make your voice heard on high. Is this the fast I have chosen? A day for one to afflict his soul? Is it to bow down his head like a reed, and spreading out sackcloth and ashes? Will you call this a fast and a day acceptable to *Adonai*?"

—Isaiah 58:3-5, TLV

Next, in Isaiah 58, the Holy One explains the fast He has chosen:

- to release the bonds of wickedness,
- to untie the cords of the yoke,
- to let the oppressed go free,
- to share your bread with the hungry,
- to bring the homeless poor into your houses,
- when you see the naked, to cover him.
- to not hide yourself from your own families.

After these things, God's people are told that their light will break forth like the dawn. Fasting is a private matter—no need to worry about whether your neighbor has repented or fed the poor.

Today, if you are a believer in Yeshua, Messiah and would like to join in the fast of Yom Kippur, do so. If you desire to pray for God's people Israel and for their eyes to be opened to Yeshua, Messiah, in their Bibles, do so.

The apostle Paul said it best:

> I am speaking to you Gentiles. Inasmuch as I am the apostle to the Gentiles, I magnify my ministry in the hope that I may provoke my own people to jealousy and save some of them.
>
> —Romans 11:13-14, BSB

The Feast of

Tabernacles

or

Sukkot

Chapter 3

The Feast of Tabernacles or Sukkot

Part 1

The Feast of Tabernacles is richly layered with sweetness and spoken of throughout our Bibles. It represents what every Believer waits for and longs for the return of the Messiah. Sukkot is a time of shouting, dancing, and jubilant joy concerning our King Yeshua and His Kingdom. The Feast of Sukkot is also known as the feast of Booths or Tabernacles. There are two places mentioned as Succoth in the Bible (Genesis 33:17) (Exodus 12:37).

Sukkot is celebrated after the Feast of Yom Kippur. After fasting and true repentance comes joy. It is the last of the foot festivals or pilgrimage festivals. Sukkot is pronounced "Sue Coat." It is also known as the Feast of Ingathering and as just simply "The Feast." In Matthew 26, the Messiah hints to the season of our joy:

But I say to you, I will not drink of this fruit of the vine from now on until that day when I drink it new with you in My Father's kingdom.

—Matthew 26:29, NASB

In ancient Israel, the people worked hard in the fields and trusted in the Holy One to send rain and bless the fruit of their labor. After the grain was grown, they had to thresh the wheat, and separate the chaff from the wheat. The grains were made ready to grind into flour. The threshing floors were outdoors, so before the rainy season came, they would gather the last of the grain and place it in their storehouses:

His winnowing fork is in His hand to thoroughly clear His threshing floor, and to gather the wheat into His barn; but He will burn up the chaff with unquenchable fire.

—Luke 3:17, NASB

Right before Sukkot, the people gathered the wheat in their storehouses, and they burned up the chaff. This is the final feast to be fulfilled after Yeshua returns for His bride.

A worldwide, multimedia, multigenerational learning platform, *Spirit & Truth,* provides Biblically based teachings, and recently an article "Threshing, Winnowing, Sieving: Separating the Good From the Bad" highlights a three-part system of threshing, winnowing, and using a sieve to get the

grain to the point where it could be ground into flour. *Spirit &
Truth* also explain that bread in ancient Israel was referred to as
a staff or walking stick. We can think of this threshing,
winnowing, and sieving as the process before and after the
Messiah returns. One portion of the blog caught my attention,
sieving:

> The woman servant—for it is only women who sift—sets
> herself on the ground with her feet spread widely apart,
> taking in her hands a large but shallow sieve
> called *ghurbal,* some two and a half feet across. Having
> placed a small amount of wheat in the *ghurbal,* or sieve,
> she commences by giving it some six or seven sharp
> shakes, so as to bring the chaff and short pieces of crushed
> straw to the surface, the greater part of which she removes
> with her hands. After this, the main part of the work
> begins, which is done with much skill. Holding the sieve
> in a slanting position, she jerks it up and down for a length
> of time, blowing across the top of it all the while with great
> force. In a word, she turns herself into a regular
> winnowing machine! [27]

In II Samuel 24 David purchases a threshing floor. This
threshing floor is the most famous threshing floor in all the
world. The story concerning the threshing floor is also told in I

---

[27] Threshing, Winnowing, Sieving: Separating the Good from the Bad | Spirit
& Truth (spiritandtruthonline.org)

Chronicles 21, where we learn that David had sinned, and God has given him three choices:

> So Gad went and said to David, "This is what the LORD says: 'You must choose between three years of famine, three months of being swept away before your enemies and overtaken by their swords, or three days of the sword of the LORD—days of plague upon the land, with the angel of the LORD ravaging every part of Israel.' "Now then, decide how I should reply to Him who sent me."
>
> —I Chronicles 21:11-12, BSB

David tells the prophet Gad to let him fall into the hand of the Holy One, for His mercies are great, but to not let him fall into the hands of men. The Holy One sent a plague upon Israel, and seventy thousand men of Israel fell dead. Afterwards, God sent an angel to destroy Jerusalem, but then stopped the angel. Curiously, David sees supernaturally into the spiritual realm. He sees the Angel standing between heaven and earth with a sword in his hand. David and the elders fell on their faces, and David cried out that he had sinned but that the sheep were innocent. The prophet Gad instructs David to build an altar on the threshing floor of Ornan the Jebusite. Ornan is also referred to as Araunah and has differing interpretations, such as Ark, joyful, or a large tree. Since King David went on to purchase the threshing floor, these names make sense considering the temple would be built here containing the Ark of the covenant, a house of joy, and a very large tree, the Tree of Life:

> Then Solomon began to build the house of the LORD in Jerusalem on Mount Moriah, where the LORD had appeared to his father David. This was the place that David had prepared on the threshing floor of Ornan the Jebusite. Solomon began construction on the second day of the second month in the fourth year of his reign.
>
> —II Chronicles 3:1-2, BSB

Solomon's temple was built on the very same threshing floor where his father David was instructed to build an altar to the Holy One. Herod's temple was on the threshing floor. This is also the location of Mount Moriah, where Abraham took his only son Isaac to sacrifice (Genesis 22). The temple was rebuilt 70 years later by the Jews when they returned from their captivity in Babylon. In 70 A.D. it was destroyed again by the Romans. Today, all that remains is the Wailing Wall. This is the same area that after the death of seventy thousand men, David then took fifty pieces of silver and paid for the property from Ornan and erected the altar. The number fifty represents the 50th year, a jubilee year in ancient Israel. The great shofar blast occurs on Yom Kippur or the Day of Atonement ten days after the Feast of Trumpets:

Then on the tenth day of the seventh month, on *Yom Kippur*, you are to sound a *shofar* blast—you are to sound the *shofar* all throughout your land. You are to make the fiftieth year holy, and proclaim liberty throughout the land to all its inhabitants. It is to be a Jubilee to you, when each of you is to return to his own property and each of you is to return to his family. That fiftieth year will be your Jubilee.

—Leviticus 25:9-11, TLV

All debt was forgiven, and all slaves were set free on the 50th year for the jubilee year. Can you picture Messiah Yeshua coming in the clouds to set up His Kingdom? This season is what leads us to the Feast of Sukkot, or Tabernacles.

The Feast of Tabernacles looks back at the Israelites who spent forty years in the wilderness living in tents or booths. Every year during this Feast many build their own makeshift tabernacle and throw a party in their Sukkah:

You shall celebrate the Feast of Booths seven days after you have gathered in from your threshing floor and your wine vat; and you shall rejoice in your feast, you and your son and your daughter and your male and female servants and the Levite and the stranger and the orphan and the widow who are in your towns. Seven days you shall celebrate a feast to the LORD your God in the place which the LORD chooses, because the LORD your God will bless you in all your produce and in all the work of your hands, so that you will be altogether joyful.

—Deuteronomy 16:13-15, CJB

During the days of Yeshua and earlier, a water libation ceremony had become part of the tradition during Sukkot. This was called the *Simchat Beit Hashoavahh* – the water-drawing festival. The priest would go to the pool of Siloam. This is the very place in John 9 that Yeshua healed a blind man. The priests would fill golden vessels with water, and they would travel through the water gate and pour out this living water so that it flowed over the altar, along with wine from other bowls. Can you see the blood and water? A picture of Yeshua's death.

The Libation Ceremony refers to Isaiah 12:

Behold, God is my salvation; I will trust, and will not be afraid; for the Lord God is my strength and my song, and he has become my salvation. "With joy, you will draw water from the wells of salvation." (Isaiah 12:2-3)." [28]

---

[28] https://www.oneforisrael.org/bible-based-teaching-from-israel/yeshua-and-the-sukkot-water-drawing-festival/

Directions are given on how to celebrate this feast in Leviticus 23. One peculiar display of rejoicing concerns waving fruit:

> On the first day you are to gather the fruit of majestic trees, the branches of palm trees, and the boughs of leafy trees and of willows of the brook. And you are to rejoice before the LORD your God for seven days. You are to celebrate this as a feast to the LORD for seven days each year. This is a permanent statute for the generations to come; you are to celebrate it in the seventh month.
>
> —Leviticus 23:40-41, BSB

One fruit mentioned is the etrog fruit. This is a yellow lemon type of produce. The instructions involve a palm branch, two willow branches, and three myrtle branches. The six branches are bound together, and the etrog is held in the other hand. This is waved towards the east, west, north, south, and up and down. But what does it all mean? I believe it is a picture of His angels gathering His elect from the four corners of the earth.

Author Stephanie Buck, a historian and author at *Timeline* was quoted in a fascinating article, titled *"This amazing date tree was grown from a seed preserved since the time of Jesus."* According to Buck, in 1963 during an excavation at Herod the Great's Palace on Masada in Israel, date palm seeds were found that dated around 2,000 years old. Some of the seeds were planted to see what would happen. One seed grew and was nicknamed "Methuselah:"

> Two thousand years later, excavators discovered that curious clay jar buried deep in hot, dry dirt. It was undisturbed and intact. Inside they found several date palm seeds. Back at the lab, scientists broke off tiny chips of the seeds' shells; carbon dating estimated their origin between 155 BC and 64 CE. Scientists preserved the seeds at Bar-Ilan University in Tel-Aviv. Forty years later, agriculture expert Dr. Elaine Solowey planted three of them. One seed sprouted. The plant would be named Methuselah, after Noah's grandfather, the oldest man in the Bible. [29]

This is the only known living date tree of its kind, for they were extinct. Methuselah lived 969 years. His name means something along the lines of, "when he dies comes sudden judgment."

> *Jones' Dictionary of Old Testament Proper Names* reads מות (*mut*) for the first part and translates the whole name with When He Is Dead It Shall Be Sent. *NOBSE*

---

[29] https://ferrelljenkins.blog/2018/05/09/

translates the whole name with Man Of A Javelin; *BDB* proposes Man Of The Dart. [30]

I find it all very fascinating! If the seed of Methuselah has been found, we are nearing the Days of Noah, but also it's been over 2,000 years since our Messiah came. Concerning the history of Methuselah, Enoch was Methuselah's father, and after he was born the Bible says Enoch began to walk with God and was no more for God took him. The Holy One told the people of that time what was to come, and although they did not know when Methuselah would die, they knew eventually he would.

The Palm branches spoken of in Leviticus 23 should remind you of one event called the triumphal entry:

> The next day, the huge crowd that had come up for the feast heard that *Yeshua* was coming to Jerusalem. So they took palm branches and went out to meet Him, shouting,
>
> "*Hoshia-na! Baruch ha-ba b'shem Adonai!*
> Blessed is He who comes in the name of the Lord!'
> The King of Israel!"
>
> Finding a young donkey, *Yeshua* sat on it, as it is written,

---

[30] Methuselah | The amazing name Methuselah: meaning and etymology (abarim-publications.com)

"Fear not, Daughter of Zion!

Look! Your King is coming,

sitting on a donkey's colt."

—John 12:12-15, TLV

God's people thought Yeshua had come to set up the Kingdom, remove them from their poverty, and rid them of the Roman tyrants who kept them in bondage. They thought He was coming as their Messiah Ben David and not as a type of Joseph. They were picturing a place where there was no more suffering or pain, but Yeshua was coming first as a spotless Lamb who did not open His mouth when led to the stake. Isaiah 42 tells us that the returning Messiah will bring justice to the nations, and He will do it without a campaign trail and apparently without even raising His voice:

> He shall not cry, nor lift up, nor cause his voice to be heard in the street. A bruised reed shall he not break, and the smoking flax shall he not quench: he shall bring forth judgment unto truth. He shall not fail nor be discouraged, till he have set judgment in the earth: and the isles shall wait for his law (Torah).
>
> —Isaiah 42:2-4, NASB

I am looking forward to this city and the King's return. Aren't you?

Many are under the impression that when the Messiah comes, we will all float up into the clouds, get a huge mansion, and walk around on streets made of gold. This is not what careful study of His Word reveals:

> Blessed is that slave whom his master finds so doing when he comes. "Truly I say to you that he will put him in charge of all his possessions.
>
> —Luke 12:43-44, NASB

The prophets Zechariah and Daniel knew about this kingdom on earth and the Messiah:

> I was watching in the night visions. Behold, One like a Son of Man, coming with the clouds of heaven. He approached the Ancient of Days and was brought into His presence. Dominion, glory and sovereignty were given to Him that all peoples, nations, and languages should serve Him.
>
> His dominion is an everlasting dominion that will never pass away, and His kingdom is one that will not be destroyed.
>
> —Daniel 7:12-14, TLV

> But the court will sit for judgment, and his dominion will be taken away, annihilated, and destroyed forever. Then

the sovereignty, the dominion and the greatness of all the kingdoms under the whole heaven will be given to the people of the saints of the Highest One; His kingdom will be an everlasting kingdom, and all the dominions will serve and obey Him.'

—Daniel 7:26-27, NASB

An everlasting kingdom of righteousness and order. Yes, this is the Sukkot of all Sukkot's.

The Father created the whole earth. It is wondrous and beautiful. Every creature from the tiniest ant to the most massive hippopotamus, every fruit tree, every mountain range, the oceans waves, wheat fields, and crimson red roses, all glorious. The Creator saw that it was good. That word *good* is *tov* in Hebrew. Meaning it worked in divine order. The Creator never said He was throwing the earth and His creation away. Something new, like a new heaven and earth, does not always mean completely new. The Bible ends where it began, in the Garden of Eden. Everything is restored to perfection as it once was. The earth was first destroyed by water, and next, it will be destroyed by fire. Once a forest is burned, it comes back with more nutrients and improves wildlife. When managed, a fire can improve the soil and create healthy green grasslands, but spiritual fire, the fire of His Ruach purifies us. In the Book of

Acts, during the Feast of Shavuot/Pentecost, fire lit on men's tongues and purified them:

> But as it is written, Eye hath not seen, nor ear heard, neither have entered into the heart of man, the things which God hath prepared for them that love him. But God hath revealed them unto us by his Spirit: for the Spirit searcheth all things, yea, the deep things of God.

> —I Corinthians 2:9-10, KJB

After the millennial reign, there will be a new heaven and a new earth. If we all lived up in the clouds in mansions, why would we need a new earth? A mansion does not excite a person very long after acquiring one. Material possessions do not have any power to bring us joy. Streets paved with gold is a metaphor for all those like Job who after suffering and great testing come forth as gold:

> But he knows the way that I take; when He has tested me, I will come forth as gold.

> —Job 23:10, NIV

This baptism of fire removes all the impurities. John the Immerser/Baptist told us plainly that he came to baptize with water, but another was coming with a baptism of fire:

In this you greatly rejoice, even though now for a little while, if necessary, you have been distressed by various trials, so that the proof of your faith, being more precious than gold which is perishable, even though tested by fire, may be found to result in praise and glory and honor at the revelation of Jesus Christ; and though you have not seen Him, you love Him, and though you do not see Him now, but believe in Him, you greatly rejoice with joy inexpressible and full of glory, obtaining as the outcome of your faith the salvation of your souls.

—I Peter 1:6-8, NASB

This gold is not in reference to shiny jewelry that the people will throw in the streets in the last days because it will be worthless. This gold represents a real, genuine humility that only comes by fire. Streets paved with gold are roads that a person walked on and suffered on, and like Job, in the midst of that suffering, the person didn't fight the fire, but let it purify them.

Remember, new does not always mean something that has never been before but instead something that is renewed. With careful reading we learn that God is coming to dwell with us:

Then I saw a new heaven and a new earth; for the first heaven and the first earth passed away, and there is no longer any sea. And I saw the holy city, New Jerusalem, coming down out of heaven from God, made ready as a bride adorned for her husband. And I heard a loud voice from the throne, saying, "Behold, the tabernacle of God is among men, and He will dwell among them, and they shall be His people, and God Himself will be among them, and He will wipe away every tear from their eyes; and there will no longer be any death; there will no longer be any mourning, or crying, or pain; the first things have passed away." And He who sits on the throne said, "Behold, I am making all things new."

—Revelation 21:1-5, NASB

The Feast of Tabernacles or Sukkot

Part 2

The majority of people celebrating Christmas today know that December 25th is not the Messiah's birthday. Regardless of when the Messiah was brought into the world, we are thankful He was. In much of the Hebrew Roots audiences it is taught that Christmas was originally a pagan holiday, corresponding to the Roman festival of Saturnalia or the feast of the sun god Sol. And in order to bring harmony, the birth of Jesus known in Hebrew as Yeshua, was placed on December 25th and would fall right next to a pagan society of festivals.

In the winter 2022 issue of *Biblical Archaeology Review*, T.C. Schmidt Yale, PhD, an assistant professor of New Testament and Early Christianity at Fairfield University, argues for an early association of Jesus's birth with December 25th in his article, *Calculating Christmas Hippolytus and December 25th*. Schmidt believes the early church felt the Messiah was born on Passover. He gives details of archeological evidence. The article states that in the Vatican Library, a statue of Hippolytus seated on a chair with an inscription from 222 AD appears on the chair's sides and back. One of the inscriptions includes a date for Jesus's conception on April 2, 2 BC. Nine months after this date would situate Jesus's birth in late December of 2 BC or early January of 1 BC. December 25 falls nicely within that range. Schmidt explains that the early Christians would have believed the Son of God was conceived on Passover and died on Passover:

> The oldest and strongest tradition, however, concerns the date of Jesus's conception, which all the earliest sources agree occurred on Passover. And this very consistency explains the diversity of calendrical dates for Jesus's birth. This is because the lunar Passover drifts back and forth between late March and mid-April. Given this, the dates for Jesus's conception (and his birth nine months later) would differ in proportion to the date which an ancient Christian chose for the Passover of Jesus's conception—for the ancients had much trouble calculating lunar phases far into the past or future and consequently often arrived at slightly different dates. This is why some ancient Christians give the date for Jesus's birth in mid-December, others December 25, and still others early January, since all those dates are about nine gestational months removed from when they each

thought the Passover of Jesus's conception happened to occur. [31]

The Chassidic masters believe that the righteous, like Moses, live their lives walking in their greatest potential for the Holy One and that they die on their birthdate. This is one of the reasons some suggest Yeshua was born on Passover and died on Passover.

Other scholars believe that the Feast of Tabernacles was the Feast our Savior and Redeemer Yeshua was born on. The Book of John states: "And the Word became flesh, and did tabernacle among us, and we beheld his glory, glory as of and only begotten of a father, full of grace and truth" (John 1:14, YLT). Yeshua did, of course, tabernacle with us, but does this solidify his birth season? I want to address each of these dates and do a brief investigation.

By following a Feast of Sukkot/Tabernacles birthdate, most researchers lean toward this season as the shepherds were still out in the fields at night with their flocks which would not have been happening in the cold and rainy season—December. The Book of Luke begins with the announcement of two pregnancies: John the Baptist's mother, Elizabeth, and Mary/Miriam, Yeshua's mother. We learn considerably from the season Elizabeth's husband's priestly order falls on and his offering of

---

[31] Calculating Christmas - The BAS Library (biblicalarchaeology.org)

incense. Zechariah was from the priestly division of Abijah. For reference, see the chart in Book One, Unveiling the Messiah in the Spring Feasts under First Fruits Part II. The course of Abijah was the 8th course in the rotation (I Chronicles 24:10). Nazarene Judaism breaks down the timeline in their article that was featured in *Plain Truth Magazine* in the Nov-Dec issue of 1985, *"Yeshua's Birth: The Untold Story."* The collection of Jewish civil and religious laws records that the first course performed its duties in the first week of the first month of Abib/Nisan (spring). The second course worked the second week, but in the third week, the festival of Passover and Unleavened Bread, all 24 courses served together. The third shift then took its turn during the fourth week of the year. Also, the quote below uses "Zacharias. The Hebrew name Zechariah (Hebrew: זְכַרְיָה), is spelled with many variations such as Zachariah and Zacharias.

Keith W. Stump of Nazarene Judaism, expounds on the birth of Messiah in his article:

> The eighth course—the course of Abijah, in which Zacharias served—worked the ninth week of the year. But Zacharias' course then stayed on at the temple to serve the 10th week also—the week of the annual Pentecost festival— along with all the other courses. It was during that two-week period of work—near the end of spring— that the announcement by the archangel Gabriel came to Zacharias regarding his wife's imminent conception

(Luke 1:8-20). Elizabeth's sixth month of pregnancy would have been in December. She would have given birth three months later—in late March or early April of the following year. Six months after that, Yeshua would have been born, in late September or early October—before the sheep were brought in from the fields, as we have seen. [32]

Going back to the Book of Luke for confirmation:

> In the days of Herod, King of Judah, there was a *kohen* [priest] named Zechariah from the **priestly division of Abijah**. Elizabeth, his wife, was from the daughters of Aaron. Together they were righteous before *Adonai*, walking without fault in all His commandments and instructions. But they were childless, because Elizabeth was barren and both of them were elderly. According to the custom of the priestly office, it became his lot to enter the Holy Place of *Adonai* to burn incense. And the whole crowd of people was praying outside at the hour of incense burning. An angel of *Adonai* appeared to him, standing at the right side of the altar of incense. Zechariah was in turmoil when he saw the angel, and fear fell upon him. But the angel said, "Do not be afraid, Zechariah, because your prayer has been heard. Your wife, Elizabeth, will give birth to your

---

[32] YESHUA'S BIRTH: The Untold Story – Nazarene Judaism

son, and you will name him John. And you will have joy and gladness, and many will rejoice at his birth.

—Luke 1:5, 6,10-14, TLV

Something interesting happens concerning Elizabeth's birth. While her husband is offering incense, an angel appears before him and tells him that his wife will become pregnant, and they will have a son who will be filled with the Holy Spirit in the power of Elijah, to turn the hearts of the fathers to their children, and the hearts of the children to their fathers. Their son will lead the people back to the fear of the Holy One, but Zechariah is a skeptic. He wants proof, and proof he receives:

"I am Gabriel, the one standing in God's presence. I was commissioned to tell you and proclaim to you this good news. So look, you will be silent and powerless to speak until the day these things happen, since you did not believe my words which will be fulfilled in their time."

When the days of his priestly service had been completed, he went home. After these days, his wife Elizabeth became pregnant and hid herself for five months, saying, "*Adonai* has done this for me! In these days He looked upon me, to take away my disgrace among the people."

—Luke 1:19-20, 23-25, TLV

Elizabeth hid herself and Zechariah was mute. Prophetically speaking, many theologians state that John was born on Passover. We know that Passover is the season of the Messiah's death as the sacrificial lamb. Certain scholars follow the pattern of the 24 courses and the order of Abijah and end up with a Sukkot birthday for the Messiah. However, the feast of Trumpets (when Yeshua returns) is close in proximity on the calendar to the Feast of Tabernacles. This feast day is mostly hidden exactly as Elizabeth was hidden for 5 months and this is the 5th feast. This feast is mainly silent, like Zechariah's inability to speak until the 8th day. The feast is a day of blowing shofars. Ten days after the Feast of Trumpets comes Yom Kippur—the Day of Atonement; then five days later, Sukkot (the Feast of Tabernacles). A number of scholars believe Yeshua's true birth occurred on Trumpets for a few reasons. This season is when Kings were crowned. If a king were elected in the month of Nisan, he would not be crowned until Rosh Hashanah, or the Feast of Trumpets. This 7th feast represents us crowning Yeshua as King overall and especially us:

> Many scholars have suggested that the first day of the seventh month was popularly celebrated in ancient Israel as a divine coronation day, the time of God's assumption of the kingship and the beginning of a new cycle of the year. There were two celebrations of a new annual cycle in ancient Israel: one in the spring month of Aviv (later

called Nisan), "the first of the months of the year" (Exodus12:2), and another in the fall at "the turn of the year" (Exodus 23:16; 34:22). [33]

Some teachings state Yeshua could not have been born during the Feast of Tabernacles because He was born in Bethlehem, not Jerusalem, and they state it was mandatory to keep the three foot festivals -- Unleavened Bread, Pentecost, and Tabernacles -- in the Land, but Bethlehem is only a few miles from the old city of Jerusalem—walking distance. However, there is nothing in the Bible that states the feasts have to be kept in the Land. Author and teacher Natan Lawerence has a lengthy article concerning this on his website Hoshana Raba, *Should we keep the biblical feasts outside the land of Israel?*

> Nowhere in the Scriptures is there a command to celebrate the feasts *only* in the land of Israel or in Jerusalem. Rather, in several places in Deuteronomy YHVH commands his people to celebrate the pilgrimage feasts where he has chosen to place his name (Deut 16:2, 6, 11). At that time, his name was where the tabernacle and latter the temple resided. However, both the tabernacle and temple are gone. Paul teaches us that the saints are YHVH's temple because his presence, in the form of the Holy Spirit, now resides in them as opposed

---

[33] The History of Rosh Hashanah, From the Torah to the Temples | My Jewish Learning

to the holy of holies in the former temple (1 Cor 3:16; 6:19). Based on this, it can reasoned that the saints can now celebrate the biblical feasts wherever YHVH leads them to do so whether in the land of Israel or not, for as Yeshua said, where two or more are gathered together in his name, he is in their midsts (Matt 18:20). Furthermore, YHVH is in the midst of his people wherever they are, for the psalmist tells us that he inhabits the praises of his people (Ps 22:3). Where YHVH is, that is where is name and anointing will be. [34]

Back to the birth of Messiah:

> Now it happened in those days a decree went out from Caesar Augustus to register all the world's inhabitants. This was the first census taken when Quirinius was governor of Syria. Everyone was traveling to be registered in his own city.
>
> —Luke 2:1-3, TLV

It is questionable that the Romans would have issued the tax during a feast day, but it is possible, and it could be the reason there were no places to rent for the night. The Gospel of Luke seems to mention a historical fact instead of a feast day. Mary

---

[34]   https://hoshanarabbah.org/blog/2014/06/03/feasts-outside-the-land-of-israel/

and Joseph were there to be registered for a Roman *census*. This is a clue, but historically hard to determine. Luke 1 states that Herod the great was ruler. The Jewish historian, Josephus, confirmed the existence of Quirinius as governor, but sited Quirinius' ruling term from AD 5 to AD 6 after the banishment of Archelaus. The Book of Matthew states that Yeshua was born during the reign of Herod the Great, but according to Josephus, the great Jewish historian, Herod died nine years prior to the governorship of Quirinius:

> Interestingly, archaeological discoveries in the nineteenth century seem to confirm Quirinius (or someone with the same name) was also proconsul of Syria and Cilicia from 11 BC to the death of Herod. Quirinius's name has been discovered on a coin from this period of time (as cited by John McRay in *Archaeology and the New Testament*) and on the base of a statue erected in Pisidian Antioch (as cited by Sir William Ramsay, *The Bearing of Recent Discovery on the Trustworthiness of the New Testament*). Quirinius may actually have ruled Syria during two separate periods and have taken two separate censuses. This is consistent with Luke's account. In Luke 2:2, Luke refers to the "first census taken while Quirinius was governor of Syria" (describing Quirinius' rule as the governor's procurator), and in Acts 5:37, Luke describes a second census taken most likely between 6-7AD (as

described by Josephus) when Quirinius was the formal governor of the region. Both Josephus and Luke link this second census to an uprising under Judas of Galilee. Only Luke's sources were present during the actual events; as a result, Luke's description of two separate censuses is reasonable. [35]

The birth of Yeshua was not when the wisemen came presenting gifts. Yeshua was a toddler at that time and lived in a house. For more on this subject, read my devotional *Jumping for Joy in the Midst of Sorrow:*

> After they had heard the king, they went on their way, and the star they had seen in the east went ahead of them until it stood over the place where the Child was. When they saw the star, they rejoiced with great delight. On coming to the house, they saw the Child with His mother Mary, and they fell down and worshiped Him. Then they opened their treasures and presented Him with gifts of gold and frankincense and myrrh.
>
> —Matthew 2:9-11, BSB

Many scholars believe that Mary/ Miriam's conception was towards the end of Kislev during Chanukah. This is usually late November to mid-December and is called the Feast of Lights or

---

[35] Unbelievable? Is Luke's Description of Quirinius Historically Inaccurate? | Cold Case Christianity

the Feast of Dedication, (John 10:22-23). Since Yeshua is the Light of the World, this season too seems acceptable. That would make John's birth during Passover. Those teaching this imply that Joseph had a year to pay his taxes, and the only reason he would travel with Mary being very pregnant was for a foot festival—Passover, Pentecost, or Sukkot/Tabernacles. This leaves them with a Sukkot birth. The greatest proof to dismiss the Sukkot birth for a Yom Teruah birth is found in the stars according to some authors and teachers. The proof text used is found in Revelation 12 concerning a woman clothed with the sun. This woman represents Israel as well as Mary or Miriam in the Hebrew.

And, one author, Ernest L. Martin, wrote a book, *The Star That Astonished the World*, and went to great lengths to prove Yeshua's birth by using the heavenly stars:

> A great sign appeared in heaven: a woman clothed with the sun, with the moon under her feet, and on her head a crown of twelve stars. She is pregnant—crying out in birth pains, in agony to give birth.
>
> Then another sign appeared in heaven: a great fiery red dragon that had seven heads and ten horns, and seven royal crowns on his heads. His tail sweeps away a third of the stars of heaven—it hurled them to the earth. Now the dragon stood before the woman who was about to give

birth, so that whenever she gave birth he might devour her child.

And she gave birth to a son, a male child, who is to rule all the nations with an iron rod. And her child was snatched away to God and to His throne. Then the woman fled into the wilderness, where she has a place prepared by God so they might take care of her for 1,260 days.

—Revelation 12:11-6, TLV

Ernest Martin states that there is only one time of year when this prophecy from Revelation 12 can occur:

The only time in the year that the Sun could be in a position to "clothe" the celestial woman called Virgo (that is, to be mid-bodied to her, in the region where a pregnant woman carries a child) is when the Sun is located between about 150 and 170 degrees along the ecliptic. This "clothing" of the woman by the Sun occurs for a 20-day period each year. This 20-degree spread could indicate the general time when Jesus was born. In 3 B.C.E., the Sun would have entered this celestial region about August 27 and exited from it about September 15. If John in the Book of Revelation is associating the birth of Jesus with the period when the Sun was mid-bodied to this woman called Virgo (and this is no doubt what he means), then Jesus would have to be born within that 20-day period.

This Virgin held in her left hand a sprig of grain. This was precisely where the bright star called Spica is found. Indeed, the chief star of the constellation Virgo is Spica.

Bullinger, in his book *The Witness of the Stars* (pp. 29–34), said that the word "Spica" has, through the Arabic, the meaning "the branch" and that it symbolically refers to Jesus who was prophetically called "the Branch" in Zechariah 3:8 and 6:12. And Bullinger (and Seiss in his book *The Gospel in the Stars*) maintains that this sign of Virgo designates the heavenly witness for the birth of the Messiah (Jesus).

Thus, the story of Jesus and his mission on earth, as related by these heavenly symbols, should logically begin with his birth from a virgin and conclude with him being crowned king in the final sign of Leo the Lion (with its chief star being Regulus — the King star). This is no doubt what the apostle John was trying to show through the symbols found in Revelation 12. [36]

Returning to the theme of a Passover birth for Yeshua, several scholars bring up the spring season for pointing to the birth of the Messiah because this is when the Passover lambs were born. The lambs for Passover had to be one year old (Ex.

---

[36] Chapter 5: The Time of Jesus' Birth (askelm.com)

12:5). They would have been born during the lambing season, the year before. Ron Cantor, in his article "When Was Yeshua Really Born?" quotes Jonathan Cahn, an American Messianic Jewish rabbi, who explains why there were shepherds in the field in the middle of the night. Cahn states that normally the shepherds would be sleeping, but because it was lambing season—the time when lambs give birth—they were out all night in case one of the mothers went into labor. Jonathan Cahn goes further and teaches that Yeshua was born on Nisan 1.

Nisan is the first month of the year, a time for new beginnings. But it would not be a time of pilgrimage or in the dead of the cold, wet winter. Cahn makes the case that every other major event in Yeshua's life and kingdom coincides with a Jewish feast day:

1. Passover—His death

2. First Fruit Offering is brought (Lev. 23) His resurrection.

3. Shavuot (Lev. 23) Birth of the church (Acts 2)

4. Rosh Hashanah— the Second Coming

5. Yom Kippur— End time forgiveness (Zech. 13:1)

6. Feast of Tabernacles— Wedding Supper of the Lamb (Is. 25, Rev. 19, Zech. 14)

    So, it makes sense that His birth would also fall on a significant day on the Jewish calendar in the spring with the other prophetic events that point to His first coming. The first of Nisan is 14 days before Passover, which begins between the 14th and 15th day of Nisan. And, it is the first day of the Jewish New Year. You may be saying, wait, I thought Rosh Hashanah was the first day of the year. Actually, the biblical name is not "New Year" but Yom Teruah, or the Feast of Trumpets. The rabbis turned it into a New Year, but it is actually the first day of the *seventh* month.

Yes, Yeshua, the Passover lamb, may have been born with other lambs just before Passover. [37]

Regardless of when our Messiah was born, we know He Lives! We believe in the power of His resurrection glory, and during Sukkot, the season of our joy, we celebrate His Kingship and His return, but Yeshua Messiah has been reigning as King for over 2,000 years. We also celebrate what will occur after this feast Sukkot that leads us to the 8th Day. In the following chapter we will explore how the 8th Day or in Hebrew, *Shemini Atzeret*, represents an amazing heavenly season of joy full to overflowing.

---

[37] When was Yeshua Really Born? (roncantor.com)

Chapter 4

Eighth Day & The Feast of Chanukah

Every week, a portion of the Torah (the first five Books of Moses) is read in Messianic and Jewish communities worldwide. The tradition of the *Haftarah* (prophets) dates back to Yeshua, who read from the book of Isaiah in the temple as recorded in Luke 4. While the portion Yeshua read is not part of the current Haftarah reading in Judaism, both Jews and Messianic congregations worldwide continue to read from the Torah and the prophets.

The reading cycle concludes with a joyous celebration known as the 8th day, following the Feast of Sukkot. This holiday, called Shemini Atzeret in Hebrew, involves dressing the Torah scrolls in regal attire with crowns and dancing in a circle with them. As we meditate on this imagery of the adorned Word and our joyful dancing, a vivid picture of the Messiah dressed in kingly robes and crowned as Lord of all emerges. This is the essence of the 8th Day celebration. The commandment for this festival is mentioned in Numbers: On the eighth day you are to hold a solemn assembly; you must not do any regular work" (Numbers 29:35, BSB). And also in Leviticus 23:

> And the LORD said to Moses, "Speak to the Israelites and say, 'On the fifteenth day of the seventh month the Feast of Tabernacles to the LORD begins, and it continues for seven days. On the first day there shall be a sacred assembly. You must not do any regular work. For seven days you are to present an offering made by fire to the LORD. On the eighth day you are to hold a sacred assembly and present an offering made by fire to the LORD. It is a solemn assembly; you must not do any regular work.'
>
> —Leviticus 23:33-36, BSB

Again, this festival is called *Simchat Torah* or *Shemini* (Eighth) *Atzeret* (Gathering). The Torah scrolls are removed from the ark and joyously paraded around the *bimah*. The *bimah* is an area with a podium in the center of the synagogue—a reading platform. This separate holiday is known in Hebrew as *Hoshanna Rabba* or in English as *The Great Hosanna*. We say *Hosanna*, but it is two words — *Hoshi* meaning to save, and *ana*, means *now. Oh, save now!* or *Please save us! Hosanna* and *Hallelujah* have two different meanings. To the first-century Jews, *Hosanna* meant to release us from our oppressors. "O LORD, save us, we pray. We beseech You, O LORD, cause us to prosper!" (Psalm 118:25, BSB). Today as tensions heat up in the world and wars rage on, along with earthquakes, floods, viruses and so forth, we cry "Save us, come Yeshua, come. Save now!"

When Yeshua makes his monumental entry riding on a donkey, the people shout for their king to deliver them. The people proclaimed Yeshua as their king and asked him to deliver them from Roman oppression. They were looking for a Savior to save them from their cruel taskmasters:

> The next day the great crowd that had come to the feast heard that Jesus was coming to Jerusalem. They took palm branches and went out to meet Him, shouting:

> "Hosanna!" "Blessed is He who comes in the name of the Lord!" "Blessed is the King of Israel!" Finding a young donkey, Jesus sat on it, as it is written: "Do not be afraid, O Daughter of Zion. See, your King is coming, seated on the colt of a donkey."

> —John 12:12-15, BSB

Can you picture a day when Yeshua Messiah returns for His Bride and dances with her like those who carry the Torah Scrolls dressed in royalty—indeed, a season of great joy! Yeshua is the Word of Truth. The Book of John says the Word became flesh and tabernacled among us, and our Messiah has returned and will return to do the same. All the feasts are about Him.

Instructions revealed in Leviticus state that on the 8th Day, the people were to offer an offering by fire to the Holy One and refrain from work. Why the command to do no work? Because we cannot save ourselves. There is no amount of trying to become good enough. "For it is by grace you have been saved through faith, and this not from yourselves; it is the gift of God, not by works, so that no one can boast" (Ephesians 2:8-9, BSB).

Only He who raised His Son from the grave can save us. The 8th-day festival is a time of dancing and gives us a glimpse of the Kingdom that's eternal—cyclical, and without end. A time when He wipes away every tear from our eyes.

What does Hanukkah have to do with the 8th Day celebration? In John 10, Yeshua enters the temple in winter during a festival called the Feast of Dedication or Hanukkah:

> At that time the Feast of the Dedication took place at Jerusalem; it was winter, and Jesus was walking in the temple in the portico of Solomon.
>
> —John 10:22-23, NASB

Being raised in Christianity, we often don't know much, if anything, about Hanukkah. As a child, all I knew was that the Jewish people lit some candles, and they exchanged eight gifts. I was busy celebrating Christmas and never really investigated this festival. The Hebrew Bible does not mention the Feast of Hanukkah, and nowhere do we read in John 10 that the Messiah celebrated it, only that He was walking around the portico.

Hannukah celebrates the rededication of the Second Temple after the Maccabean Revolt. The primary source for information on it is in 1 Maccabees 4:36-59. In 164 BCE, "Judas (Maccabaeus) and his brothers and the entire assembly of Israel declared that every year for eight days, from the twenty-fifth day of Kislev, the days of the dedication of the [newly rebuilt] altar should be observed with joy and gladness on the anniversary." (1 Macc.4:59, NABRE). [38]

Notice in John 10 that it was winter, so it fell after the fall Feast, The Feast of Trumpets, The Day of Atonement, and The Feast of Tabernacles, Sukkot. Also from John 10, we learn that Yeshua on Hanukkah was in a specific part of the temple—Solomon's porch. This portico is mentioned throughout the Bible and was also the place of judgment. In Acts 3, Peter and John enter the temple during the hour of prayer, and they see a man lying at the gate begging for alms. The man is healed at this specific place, Solomon's Portico:

> And all the people saw him walking and praising God, and they were taking note of him as being the one who used to sit at the Beautiful Gate of the temple to beg alms, and

---

[38]

https://www.reddit.com/r/AcademicBiblical/comments/17pwev6/historical_hanukkah_narrative/

they were filled with wonder and amazement at what had happened to him. While he was clinging to Peter and John, all the people ran together to them at the so-called portico of Solomon, full of amazement.

—Acts 3:9-11, NASB

In Acts 5, we read more concerning this area or portico of the temple that is still standing today:

At the hands of the apostles many signs and wonders were taking place among the people; and they were all with one accord in Solomon's portico.

—Acts 5:12, NASB

Again, we see miracles, signs, and wonders happening at Solomon's porch or colonnade, and everyone is in one accord. Triple gates are located where Solomon's portico was built on the east wall.

Author of *Locating Solomon's Temple* and *The Temple Mount*, Norma Robertson writes in her article titled "Solomon's Porch-Portico" that the early church met on Solomon's Porch (Acts 5:12). The portico was the scene of Yeshua's teaching at the Festival of Hanukkah. Robertson quotes James Barclay, who explored and made diagrams of the Triple Gate in 1844. Robertson believes *The House of the Forest of Lebanon* also contained Solomon's Porch of Judgment. The author references that this house was probably an Armory because Solomon stored

200 solid gold targets, a shield large enough to cover a man when kneeling on one knee, and also 300 solid gold shields. She quotes several sources, such as Sir Charles Warren, a British Royal Engineer and one of the earliest European archaeologists of the Biblical Holy Land:

> Sir Charles Warren writes that M. DeSaulcy is said to have discovered, in the drain beneath the Triple Gate, an inscription in Hebrew that reads, *'Here let every man keep silence.'* [39]

> When the Lamb opened the seventh seal, there was silence in heaven for about half an hour.

> —Revelation 8:1, ESV

Could this be a symbol or sign of the judgment Seat? The name Solomon means recompense, completeness, and peace. This sounds much like our Messiah, the Prince of Peace who will come and bring recompense. I Kings 7 gives more details concerning this House of judgment:

> [Solomon]He built the House of the Forest of Lebanon a hundred cubits long, fifty cubits wide, and thirty cubits high, with four rows of cedar pillars supporting the cedar beams. The house was roofed with cedar above the beams

---

[39] https://www.jewishvirtuallibrary.org/warren-sir-charles-x00b0

that rested on the pillars—forty-five beams, fifteen per row. There were three rows of high windows facing one another in three tiers. All the doorways had rectangular frames, with the openings facing one another in three tiers. Solomon made his colonnade fifty cubits long and thirty cubits wide, with a portico in front of it and a canopy with pillars in front of the portico.

In addition, he built a hall for the throne, the Hall of Justice, where he was to judge. It was paneled with cedar from floor to ceiling.

—I Kings 7:2-7, BSB

Even more astounding than the hall of justice is what the Jewish Historian Josephus had to say about the portico area:

Herod did not rebuild Solomon's porch, called the eastern cloisters. The workers wanted to rebuild the eastern cloisters. The request was denied. A portion of the temple which according to Josephus remained from Solomon's time. These cloisters belonged to the outer court, (woman's court) and were situated in a deep valley, and had walls that reached four hundred cubits [in length] (600 feet in Herod's time), and were built of square and very white stones, the length of each of which stones was twenty cubits, and their height six cubits. This was the

work of King Solomon, who first built the entire temple."
40

The Day of Judgment will happen for the whole world. Messiah Yeshua may render a judgment there at Solomon's porch, but perchance not as we have understood it:

> Therefore, whether at home or away from home, we try our utmost to please him; for we must all appear before the Messiah's court of judgment, where everyone will receive the good or bad consequences of what he did while he was in the body.
>
> —II Corinthians 5:9-10, CJB

Is this what we felt in our spirit when we ran to an altar or fell on our faces in repentance? Or is this pointing us to Messiah's judgment? This portico is a place of reward as well. The Eastern gate is where the Messiah will enter — also known as the King's gate:

> Then He brought me back by the way of the outer gate of the sanctuary, which faces the east; and it was shut. The LORD said to me, "This gate shall be shut; it shall not be opened, and no one shall enter by it, for the LORD God of Israel has entered by it; therefore it shall be shut. As for the prince, he shall sit in it as prince to eat bread before

---

40 https://www.ccel.org/ccel/josephus/complete.iii.vi.v.html

the LORD; he shall enter by way of the porch of the gate and shall go out by the same way."

—Ezekiel 44:1-3, NASB

We also learn that the Messiah will come through the Eastern gate in Psalms 24:

Lift up your heads, O gates, and be lifted up, O ancient doors, that the King of glory may come in! Who is the King of glory? The LORD strong and mighty, the LORD mighty in battle. Lift up your heads, O gates, and lift them up, O ancient doors, that the King of glory may come in!

—Psalm 24:7-9, NASB

The present Eastern Gate is located on the eastern wall of the Old City, opposite the Mount of Olives, also known as the Mount of Anointing, the Mount of Messiah:

In A.D. 70 the Romans destroyed the gate. In A.D. 629 a ceremonial gate was constructed to receive a Byzantine emperor who allegedly was returning the "true cross" stolen by the Persians in 614. Later, during the Crusader period, the Muslims sealed the gate, ostensibly for security reasons. Yet some Jewish people feel the Muslims believed it would prevent the Messiah from entering. The present sealed gate was the work of the Ottoman Sultan Suleiman in 1538.

According to Bible prophecy and tradition, the Messiah will come from the east of Jerusalem (Zech. 14:4). It was also taught He would ride in on a donkey (Zech. 9:9). The general understanding has been that Messiah will enter the Temple through the Eastern Gate. Thus this gate became associated with Messianic anticipation. [41]

The Book of Ezekiel hints to this shut gate that Yeshua went through on a humble donkey:

> The man then brought me back to the outer gate of the sanctuary that faced east, but it was shut. And the LORD said to me, "This gate is to remain shut. It shall not be opened, and no man shall enter through it, because the LORD, the God of Israel, has entered through it. Therefore it will remain shut. Only the prince himself may sit inside the gateway to eat in the presence of the LORD. He must enter by way of the portico of the gateway and go out the same way."
>
> —Ezekiel 44:1-3, BSB

A large wall with many gates surrounds the Old City of Jerusalem: the Jaffa Gate, Zion Gate, and the Dung Gate. The Dung Gate takes one to the Western Wall, where the Jewish people pray. Continuing is the Damascus Gate and the Golden Gate. The Eastern Gate, known as the Beautiful Gate or the

---

[41] The Eastern Gate – Israel My Glory

Golden Gate, faces the Mount of Olives. This gate is unique, as it is sealed shut:

> The Eastern Gate is the only gate from the east leading directly into what used to be the Jewish temple complex.
>
> The gate is part of the city wall rebuilt from 1537 to 1541 by Sultan Suleiman I of the Ottoman Empire. It is believed this is the site of the Gate Beautiful mentioned in Acts 3:2. When Jerome translated the Greek New Testament into Latin (386 A.D.), he translated the Greek word "*oraia*" (beautiful), into the Latin "*aurea*" (golden). Thus the Eastern Gate came to us as The Golden Gate instead of The Gate Beautiful. [42]

Will the Messiah come through this gate? Only time will tell, but prophecy suggests that this gate will remain shut until the Messiah enters it again. According to Ezekiel, more than likely during the fall feasts.

The fall feasts begin with the Feast of Trumpets or Yom Teruah—a day of blowing. This is the 5th feast, which many believe is when Yeshua's return will come. The second set apart day is the Day of Atonement or the judgment seat. Then, the 7th feast, Sukkot or Feast of Tabernacles, is when believers rule and reign with the Messiah. Following the end of this feast is the 8th

---

[42] Must Ezekiel 44:1-3 be fulfilled prior to the new Eden of Revelation 22? - Biblical Hermeneutics Stack Exchange

Day. There is a similar time in Revelation when the Father makes everything NEW. This comes after the seven-year tribulation and judgment:

> And He who sits on the throne said, "Behold, I am making all things new." And He said, "Write, for these words are faithful and true." Then He said to me, "It is done. I am the Alpha and the Omega, the beginning and the end. I will give to the one who thirsts from the spring of the water of life without cost. He who overcomes will inherit these things, and I will be his God, and he will be My son. But for the cowardly and unbelieving and abominable and murderers and immoral persons and sorcerers and idolaters and all liars, their part will be in the lake that burns with fire and brimstone, which is the second death."
>
> —Revelation 21:5-8, NASB

This passage from Revelation 21 describes joy unspeakable and full of glory for those who overcome. We become new creatures, drinking from the fountain of life, and living forever with our Father and His Son, the Lamb. However, the second death will come upon the others mentioned in Revelation 21, the sorcerers, the liars, the idolaters. That day will be the worst feeling a soul has ever felt in this lifetime or the one to come. Such dreadful sorrow indeed—sorrow that causes one's teeth to gnash:

There shall be there the weeping and the gnashing of the teeth, when ye may see Abraham, and Isaac, and Jacob, and all the prophets, in the reign of God, and yourselves being cast out without.

—Luke 13:28, YLT

How blessed are those who wash their robes, so that they have the right to eat from the Tree of Life and go through the gates into the city!

—Revelation 22:14, CJB

To understand this 8th Day better, Kisha Gallagher, author of *Grace in Torah,* in her blog "Hebrew Numbers 1—10," defines the meaning of the number 8 in Hebrew;

Shemoni [f.], shemonah [m.] Literally to "make fat." New beginnings, not just complete (like seven), but satiated. Becoming "fat" is having more than enough. Full to overflowing. Moves from natural to supernatural. Transcends natural time and space to supernatural realm. Figuratively, eight takes one through a full cycle of seven, and begins anew – the One Day – Yom Echad – of creation. But, it also alludes to greater authority (doubled 4), accountability, and holiness (set apartness). [43]

---

[43] Hebrew Numbers 1-10 | GRACE in TORAH

These new beginnings are outside of time. This is a supernatural realm we cannot experience without the Holy One's presence. It is compared to the Garden of Eden before man sinned.

In the Book of John, Chapter 20, Yeshua appears to his disciples, and he breathes on them and tells them to receive the Holy Spirit/Ruach. In the New Testament, one of the disciples named Thomas gives clues to what the 8th day may symbolize.

> But Thomas, one of the twelve, called Didymus, was not with them when Jesus came. So the other disciples were saying to him, "We have seen the Lord!" But he said to them, "Unless I see in His hands the imprint of the nails, and put my finger into the place of the nails, and put my hand into His side, I will not believe." After eight days His disciples were again inside, and Thomas with them. Jesus came, the doors having been shut, and stood in their midst and said, "Peace be with you." Then He said to Thomas, "Reach here with your finger, and see My hands; and reach here your hand and put it into My side; and do not be unbelieving, but believing." Thomas answered and said to Him, "My Lord and my God!" Jesus said to him, "Because you have seen Me, have you believed? Blessed are they who did not see, and yet believed."
>
> —John 20:24-29, NASB

Notice, in John 20, Yeshua appears to them after eight days and also the doors had been shut. In Matthew 25, there are five wise virgins and five foolish who all fall asleep until the shofar sounds. Interestingly, the foolish, who must travail and bring more oil, cannot enter as a door has been shut:

> Then all the virgins woke up and trimmed their lamps. The foolish ones said to the wise, "Give us some of your oil; our lamps are going out."
>
> "No," said the wise ones, "or there may not be enough for both us and you. Instead, go to those who sell oil and buy some for yourselves." But while they were on their way to buy it, the bridegroom arrived. Those who were ready went in with him to the wedding banquet, and the door was shut. Later the other virgins arrived and said, "Lord, lord, open the door for us!"
>
> But he replied, "Truly I tell you, I do not know you." Therefore keep watch, because you do not know the day or the hour.
>
> —Matthew 25:7-13, BSB

This eighth day is connected to a future time when we will see Him with our eyes opened as Thomas did, but we must keep our oil lamps trimmed and full. This is reminiscent of the golden Menorah lamp: "Then the LORD said to Moses, "Command the

Israelites to bring you pure oil of pressed olives for the light, to keep the lamps burning continually" (Leviticus 24:1-2, BSB).

After the Feast of Trumpets is the Day of Atonement (Judgement) and then the Feast of Tabernacles or Sukkot which represents when we rule and reign with the Messiah. After Sukkot we have *Shemini Atzeret*—the eighth day:

> On the eighth day you are to hold a sacred assembly and present an offering made by fire to the LORD. It is a solemn assembly; you must not do any regular work.
>
> —Leviticus 23:36, BSB

> On the eighth day you shall have a solemn assembly; you shall do no laborious work.
>
> —Numbers 29:35, NASB

Rabbis teach that on this eighth day we reach a place of the purest joy ever known. They claim it is a river of refreshment, and a time of unspeakable joy we have never felt before. This is a time we all long for. This time is spoken of by the Revelator John when the Father of Glory will wipe away our tears and there will no longer be death, mourning, or pain:

> And the One seated upon the throne said, "Behold, I am making all things new!" Then He said, "Write, for these words are trustworthy and true." Then He said to me, "It is done! I am the Alpha and the Omega, the Beginning and

the End. To the thirsty I will freely give from the spring of the water of life.

—Revelation 21:5-7, TLV

The Holy One is making all things new, outside of time and overflowing with living water and great joy!

Unveiling the Messiah in the Fall Feasts

Closing

The significance of the feasts listed in Leviticus 23 cannot be denied. These feasts provide profound insights that bring our Bibles to life. The prophetic feasts reveal the journey of the Messiah as the spotless Lamb of God who takes away the sins of the world during Passover. We understand that He was and is the sinless Bread of Life, buried in the heart of the earth for three days and nights. The Messiah arose from the grave on First Fruits, and after ministering for 40 days, He ascended on High and instructed the Apostles to wait for the promise. They were counting up to 50 (Pentecost/Shavuot) for the outpouring of the Ruach HaKodesh, the Holy Spirit. Then, as recorded in the Book of Acts, over 3,000 souls were brought back into the covenant.

After the spring feasts such as Passover, Unleavened Bread, First Fruits, and Shavuot, the fall feasts begin. Similar to a rehearsal for a play, we eagerly anticipate the curtain call and the blowing of shofars as we wait for our returning King, keeping our eyes on the heavens. We strive to be prepared by praying and engaging in acts of righteousness, like trimming our wicks and refilling our oil lamps daily.

We begin this book with Abraham and his son, Isaac. Abraham is prepared to offer his son as a sacrifice, and Isaac is willing to die. The Holy One calls from the heavens and stops Abraham before the knife penetrates Isaac. At the beginning of the story, Abraham hears the Voice of Adonai and says, "hineni." Author Avital Snow of Firm Fellowship of Israel explains why this utterance is so powerful in his article "Here am I! – the Hebrew meaning of Hineni:"

> What makes "hineni" such a powerful statement? It is an offer of complete availability, of total readiness to serve. When we utter "hineni", we make ourselves fully available to whatever it is God might ask of us. Even without knowing what that might be. The answer of "hineni" is one of faith. [44]

In the Genesis account of Abraham and Isaac, a ram is caught in a thicket of thorns. This is a picture of the Messiah's bloody crown at the crucifixion. Natan Lawrence, a biblical Hebrew scholar who hosts a blog *Hashana Rabbah, Midrash*, explains the ram's horn in detail and a prophetic look at the coming King in his article, "The 'Sacrifice' of Isaac at Mount Moriah:"

> In Hebraic thought and prophetically-speaking, the left horn of the ram signifies mercy and grace. This is also a

---

[44] https://firmisrael.org/learn/here-am-i-the-hebrew-meaning-of-hineni/

picture of the left (or weaker) hand of YHVH, which symbolizes grace, or the feminine side of Elohim. Furthermore, the left horn of the redemptive ram signifies the purpose of the first coming of Messiah Yeshua as the Suffering Savior, as one bringing mercy and grace, and who refused to quench a smoking flax or breaking a bruised reed as a meek and quiet lamb going to its slaughter (Matt 12:20; John 12:47; Isa 53:7). The right horn of the ram caught in the thicket represents judgment picturing Elohim's stronger right hand of power, might and judgment (Ps 89:10,13–14). Thus, this horn represents the second coming of Messiah, who is seated at the right hand of the Father (Acts 2:32–33), and who will come this time in power as King of kings to rule with a rod of iron and to judge the living and the dead, and to destroy all his enemies (Rev 17:14; 19:15). [45]

According to the rabbis and Natan, the left horn of the ram is sounded on Shavuot, representing the grace of our Father and His mercies which are made new each morning. The right horn is Yahweh's strong Right Hand and at the return of His Son, Yeshua Messiah, this horn will send a loud cry throughout the world—the *Tekia Gadolah*. The Lion of Judah will roar and

---

[45] https://hoshanarabbah.org/blog/2018/10/27/sacrifice-of-isaac-at-mount-moriah/

separate the sheep from the goats at the judgment seat. Those who wash and dress in robes of righteousness will shine like the stars in the heavens. May we be ready, with our wicks trimmed and our lamps lit, knowing the seasons and awaiting His return.

Unveiling The Messiah In The Fall Feasts examines each Feast or Moedim with prophetic insight, simplicity, and understanding, and reveals the beauty of finding the Messiah hidden in each one. We discovered that the feasts are Adonai's feasts, as He says repeatedly, "These are my Feasts!" "Speak to the Israelites and say to them, 'These are My appointed feasts, the feasts of the LORD that you are to proclaim as sacred assemblies" (Leviticus 23:2, BSB).

The Prophetic Feasts of Adonai are not difficult. Keeping Christmas or Easter can be a lot of work, even for those who enjoy baking, trimming a tree, dyeing eggs, decorating, and shopping for people. The Passover meal, on the other hand, is not hard, and it's all about our King Yeshua. Each feast brings joy and is a gift to us from the Father.

I leave you with the words of Paul, the apostle, to the church in Thessalonians. Paul explains the heavenly clock and calendar and how we can know the season of our Messiah's return—not the day nor the hour, which only the Father knows, not even the Son, but we can know the seasons:

> Now concerning the times and seasons, brothers and sisters, you have no need for anything to be written to

you. For you yourselves know very well that the Day of the Lord comes like a thief in the night. When they are saying, "*Shalom* and safety," sudden destruction comes upon them like a woman having birth pains in the womb—there is no way they will escape. But you, brothers and sisters, are not in the dark, so that the Day might overtake you like a thief. For you all are sons of light and sons of day. We are not of night or of darkness — so then, let us not sleep as the others do, but let us remain alert and sober-minded. For those who sleep, sleep at night; and those who get drunk, get drunk at night. But since we are of the day, let us be sober-minded—putting on the breastplate of faithfulness and love, and the hope of salvation as a helmet. For God did not destine us for wrath but for obtaining salvation through our Lord *Yeshua* the Messiah. He died for us so that, whether we may be awake or asleep, we may live together with Him. Therefore encourage one another and build each other up—just as you in fact are doing.

—I Thessalonians 5:1-11, TLV

Blessings,

Tekoa Manning

DON'T GO YET

Thank you for reading *Unveiling the Messiah in the Fall Feasts*. If you haven't already, I hope you will read the first book on the Feasts, *Unveiling the Messiah in the Spring Feasts*. These books have been a labor of love and have taken years of research to complete. Your feedback and thoughts are important to me.

COULD YOU HELP ME?

Please leave me an honest review on Amazon or Goodreads. It would mean so much to me, and the proceeds will help us provide financial support to orphans and widows in India and Malawi.

Please refer these books to those who you believe may benefit. Also, check out my new series, *Unmasking the Unseen*. For updates and new book releases, go to Tekoamanning.com. Follow my author page on Amazon, Goodreads, and Facebook.

Blessings & Shalom,
Tekoa Manning
Manning the Gate Publishing LLC

Sources

1. Jewish Virtual Library, Ancient Jewish History: *The Great Revolt* (66 - 70 CE) (No date) Retrieved on 5-3-2024. https://www.jewishvirtuallibrary.org/the-great-revolt-66-70-ce

2. Byrd, Deborah, Sessions, Larry, EarthSky, *Spica, the bright beacon of Virgo, is 2 stars* (5-19-2024) Retrieved on 5-25-2024. https://earthsky.org/brightest-stars/speed-on-to-spica-the-15th-brightest-star/

3. Patterson, Susan, Off The Grid News, *God's Dietary Laws: Why Pigs, Crabs And Lobsters Are Bad For You.* (No Dates). Retrieved 5-1-2024. https://www.offthegridnews.com/off-grid-foods/gods-dietary-laws-why-pigs-crabs-and-lobsters-are-bad-for-you/

4. Patterson, Susan, Off The Grid News, *God's Dietary Laws: Why Pigs, Crabs And Lobsters Are Bad For You.* (No Dates). Retrieved 5-1-2024. https://www.offthegridnews.com/off-grid-foods/gods-dietary-laws-why-pigs-crabs-and-lobsters-are-bad-for-you/

5. Shaunak, Aran, Food Unfolded, *Cleaning The Seas with Mussel and Oyster Farms. (1-14-2024). Retrieved on 5-3-2024). https://www.foodunfolded.com/article/cleaning-the-seas-with-mussel-and-oyster-farms#ref6*

6. Sanhedrin Dictionary, Babylonian Talmud: Tractate Sanhedrin, Folio 97a. (No dates) Retrieved on 5-4-2024. http://www.come-and-hear.com/sanhedrin/sanhedrin_97.html

7. O'Dell, Bob, Ariel, Gidon, Israel 365 News, *The Mystery of the Lost Jubilee: Part XX – 6000 Years Old?* (6-1-2016) Retrieved 1-24-2022. https://israel365news.com/307706/the-mystery-of-the-lost-jubilee-part-xx-6000-years-old-opinion/

8. Tolle Lege, *On the day called Sunday" by Justin Martyr (A.D. 110-165)* (1-29-2009). Retrieved on 1-30-2022. https://tollelege.net/2009/01/29/on-the-day-called-sunday-by-justin-martyr-ad-110-165/

9. Fausset, Andrew Robert M.A., D.D., *Definition for 'tares' Fausset's Bible Dictionary,* (No Dates) Retrieved on 2-12-2022, *https://bible-history.com/faussets/t/tares/*

10. Moen, Skip, Dr, Hebrew Word Study, *The "Rapture" Monkey Wrench,* (8-21-2017) Retrieved on 3-14-2022. https://skipmoen.com/2017/08/the-rapture-monkey-wrench/

11. Biblical Eschatology Blog, *The History of the Rapture,* (12-4-2008) Retrieved on 8-21-2022. https://biblicaleschatology.org/2008/12/04/the-history-of-the-rapture/

12. Bible Hub, I Thessalonians 4, Greek, Commentary. (No dates) Retrieved on 8-25-2022. https://biblehub.com/interlinear/1_thessalonians/4.htm

13. Williamson, Thomas, Biblical Examiner, *Time of Jacob's Trouble - Future or Fulfilled?* (No dates) Retrieved on 6-25-2024. http://biblicalexaminer.org/W_Jacob%27s%20Troubles.html

14. Abarim Publication, *Edom in Biblical Hebrew* (No dates) Retrieved on 7-1-2024. https://www.abarim-publications.com/Meaning/Edom.html

15. Gallagher, Kisha, Grace In Torah, Hebrew Numbers 1-10, (6-15-2015) Retrieved on 6-25-2024. https://graceintorah.net/2015/06/15/hebrew-numbers-1-10/

16. Tanner, Paul, J. BIBLIOTHECA SACRA, *is Daniel's Seventy-Weeks Prophecy Messianic? Part 2,* (July-September 2009) Retrieved 7-3-2024. https://paultanner.org/English%20HTML/Publ%20Articles/Daniel%27s%2070th%20Wk%20-%20BibSac%20Article%202%20-%20Dr%20Tanner.pdf

17. My Jewish Learning, The Yom Kippur Confession (Viddui) (No dates) Retrieved on 9-1-2022. https://www.myjewishlearning.com/article/confession-vidui/

18. Tillian, Tricia, Banner Ministries, *Why Half An Hour's Silence in Heaven?* (4-20-2015) Retrieved on 10-19-2021. https://bannerministries.wordpress.com/2015/04/20/why-half-an-hours-silence-in-heaven/

19. Jastrow, Morris, Jr., McCurdy, Frederic, J., Kohler, Kaufann, Jastrow, Marcus, Husik, Isaac, Jewish Encyclopedia, Azazel, (Scapegoat, Lev. xvi., A. V.) (No dates) Retrieved on 2-12-2022. https://www.jewishencyclopedia.com/articles/2203-azazel

20. Bible Hub Strong's Concordance, 579, Anah, (No dates) Retrieved 7-3-2024. https://biblehub.com/hebrew/579.htm

21. Abarim Publications, Barabbas in Biblical Greek. (No Dates). Retrieved on 7-14-2024. https://www.abarim-publications.com/Meaning/Barabbas.html

22. Sumner, Paul, Hebrew Streams, *Yeshua bar Abba and Barabbas,* (No dates) Retrieved on 7-14-2024. https://www.hebrew-streams.org/works/ntstudies/yeshua-bar-abba.html

23. Yoma 39A, The Wiliam Davidson Talmud. (No dates) Retrieved on 7-14-2024. https://www.hebrew-streams.org/works/ntstudies/yeshua-bar-abba.html

24. Federoff, N., Peterson, T., Window View, *Talmudic Evidence for the Messiah at 30 C.E.* (No dates). Retrieved on 7-14, 2024. https://windowview.org/hmny/pgs/talmuds.30ce.html

25. Josephus, Flavius, The Complete Works. CHAPTER 5. THE GREAT DISTRESS THE JEWS WERE IN UPON THE CONFLAGRATION OF THE HOLY HOUSE. CONCERNING A FALSE PROPHET, AND THE SIGNS THAT PRECEDED THIS DESTRUCTION. (No dates) Retrieved on 7-14-2024. https://ccel.org/ccel/josephus/complete.iii.vii.v.html

26. Scott, Brad, Wildbranch Ministry, *Womb.* (No date) Retrieved on 6-1-2024. *https://www.wildbranch.org/teachings/word-studies/32womb.html*

27. Spirit and Truth Educational Platform, *Threshing, Winnowing, Sieving: Separating the Good from the Bad* (3-21-2014) Retrieved on 5-12-2022.
https://spiritandtruthonline.org/threshing-winnowing-sieving-separating-the-good-from-the-bad/

28. One For Israel, *Yeshua and the Sukkot Water Drawing Festival* (no dates) Retrieved on 6-12-2024.
https://www.oneforisrael.org/bible-based-teaching-from-israel/yeshua-and-the-sukkot-water-drawing-festival/

29. *Ferrell's Travel Blog, The Arabah – Keturah, the home of Methuselah, (5-9-2018). Retrieved on 4-12-2022.*
https://ferrelljenkins.blog/2018/05/09/

30. Abarim Publication, *Methuselah in Biblical Hebrew* (No dates) retrieved on 5-9-2018. https://www.abarim-publications.com/Meaning/Methuselah.html

31. *Schmidt, T. C., Biblical Archaeology Society Library, Calculating Christmas: Hippolytus and December 25th.* (2022) Retrieved on 5-12-2024.
https://library.biblicalarchaeology.org/article/calculating-christmas/

32. Stump, Keith, W., Nazarene Judaism, Yeshua's Birth, The Untold Story, Originally Published in Plain Truth Magazine Nov-Dec 1985 (No Dates) Retrieved on 1-23-2024.
https://nazarenejudaism.com/?page_id=613

33. Rabbi Hammer, Reuven, Dr. My Jewish Learning, *The History of Rosh Hashanah, From the Torah to the Temple.* (No date) Retrieved on 5-9-2018.
https://www.myjewishlearning.com/article/rosh-hashanah-from-the-torah-to-the-temples/

34. Lawrence, Natan, Hoshana Rabbah, *Should we keep the biblical feasts outside the land of Israel?* (6-3-2014) Retrieved on 7-5-2024.
https://hoshanarabbah.org/blog/2014/06/03/feasts-outside-the-land-of-israel/

35. Wallace, Warner, J., Cold Case Christianity, *Unbelievable? Is Luke's Description of Quirinius Historically Inaccurate?* (8-16-2017). Retrieved on 6-16-2024.
https://coldcasechristianity.com/writings/unbeliev able-is-lukes-description-of-quirinius-historically-inaccurate/

36. Corder, Charlie, Associates for Spiritual Knowledge, *The Time of Jesus' Birth,* (No date) Retrieved on 6-16, 2024.
https://www.askelm.com/star/star006.htm

37. Cantor, Ron, Israel in Crisis, *When was Yeshua Really Born?* (12-22-2018) Retrieved on 6-16-2024.
https://www.roncantor.com/post/when-was-yeshua-really-born

38. R/Academic Biblical, Reddit, Qumrun 60, *Historical Hanukkah narrative?* (11-1-2023) Retrieved on 7-19-2024.
https://www.reddit.com/r/AcademicBiblical/comments/17 pwev6/historical_hanukkah_narrative/

39. Begg, P, Jack the Ripper: The Definitive History. Jewish Virtual Library, *Sir Charles Warren,* (2003) Retrieved on 7-12-2024. https://www.jewishvirtuallibrary.org/warren-sir-charles-x00b0#google_vignette

40. Christian Classics Ethereal Library, *Josephus: The Complete Works.*, (No date) Retrieved on 6-19-2024.
https://ccel.org/ccel/josephus/complete/complete.

41. Colón, Peter, Israel My Glory, *The Eastern Gate,* (10-11-2004) Retrieved on 7-22-2024.
https://israelmyglory.org/article/the-eastern-gate/

42. Stack Exchange, Biblical Hermeneutics, *Must Ezekiel 44:1-3 be fulfilled prior to the new Eden of Revelation 22?* (7-14-2020) Retrieved on 7-11-2024.
https://hermeneutics.stackexchange.com/questions/50394/must-ezekiel-441-3-be-fulfilled-prior-to-the-new-eden-of-revelation-22

43. Gallagher, Kisha, Grace in Torah Numbers, *Hebrew Numbers 1-10* (6-15-2015). Retrieved on 7-12-2024.
https://graceintorah.net/2015/06/15/hebrew-numbers-1-10/

44. Snow, Avital, Firm Fellowship of Israel, *Here am I! – the Hebrew meaning of Hineni. (10-19-2021) Retrieved on 7-14-2024. https://firmisrael.org/learn/here-am-i-the-hebrew-meaning-of-hineni/*

45. Lawrence, Natan, Hoshana Rabbah, *The "Sacrifice" of Isaac at Mount Moriah and Yeshua the Messiah.* (10-27-2018). Retrieved on 7-7-2024.
https://hoshanarabbah.org/blog/2018/10/27/sacrifice-of-isaac-at-mount-moriah/

www.ingramcontent.com/pod-product-compliance
Lightning Source LLC
Chambersburg PA
CBHW061154120626
46546CB00005B/2058